Third Workshop on NLP Applications to Field Linguistics (FieldMatters 2024)

AA001685

Bangkok, Thailand
16 August 2024

ISBN: 979-8-3313-0162-0

Printed from e-media with permission by:

Curran Associates, Inc.
57 Morehouse Lane
Red Hook, NY 12571

Some format issues inherent in the e-media version may also appear in this print version.

Copyright© (2024) by the Association for Computational Linguistics
All rights reserved.

Printed with permission by Curran Associates, Inc. (2025)

For permission requests, please contact the Association for Computational Linguistics at the address below.

Association for Computational Linguistics
209 N. Eighth Street
Stroudsburg, Pennsylvania 18360

Phone: 1-570-476-8006
Fax: 1-570-476-0860

acl@aclweb.org

Additional copies of this publication are available from:

Curran Associates, Inc.
57 Morehouse Lane
Red Hook, NY 12571 USA
Phone: 845-758-0400
Fax: 845-758-2633
Email: curran@proceedings.com
Web: www.proceedings.com

FieldMatters 2024

Field Matters. The Third Workshop on NLP Applications to Field Linguistics

Proceedings of the Workshop

August 16, 2024

©2024 Association for Computational Linguistics

Association for Computational Linguistics (ACL)
317 Sidney Baker St. S
Suite 400 - 134
Kerrville, TX 78028
USA
Tel: +1-855-225-1962
acl@aclweb.org

Preface

Field Matters is a workshop focused on the various applications of NLP methods to field linguistics and the analysis of field data.

The primary pursuit of linguistic fieldwork is to document and describe languages. The former typically involves building a corpus and other resources for the language community, the latter ideally aims to produce a reference grammar. Advances in technology have enabled vast quantities of media to be recorded. These recordings (sound and/or video) require annotation and analysis for further linguistic research or resource development. This is often done manually. This processing bottleneck can be significantly sped up with computational methods.

NLP research focuses on developing methodology for different tasks that show significant performance in high-resource languages, allowing the automation of various routine tasks. The processing burdens faced by field linguists present a natural opportunity to marry NLP practices with the workflow of a field linguist. Similarly, the future development of NLP methods could gain from the linguistic diversity and unique tasks encountered during the description/documentation efforts.

With these in mind, Field Matters aims to provide a platform to deepen the dialogue between Computational and Field Linguists. Our workshop is hosted by the 62nd Annual Meeting of the Association for Computational Linguistics.

To highlight the highly interdisciplinary nature of our aim we invite field linguists and NLP researchers worldwide to our program committee. Each paper was assigned a field linguist along side minimally two computational linguists. Analyzing the difference in reviews of field linguists and NLP researchers, we have seen that reviewers provide different perspectives and give more diverse and fruitful feedback: while field linguists pay attention how practical this application could be or how well it fits in the idea of the workshop, NLP specialists comment on how relevant and accurate chosen methods are.

After the hard process of reviewing all submissions, the program committee chose nine papers for a poster or oral presentation at the workshop. Accepted papers illustrate the main idea of our workshop: how field linguistics may benefit from using contemporary methods of computational analysis and how the NLP community may evolve its methods with the help of under-resourced languages.

More specifically, chosen papers cover the following topics:

- Tools for fieldwork, including a language documentation tool and guidelines for human-computer interaction in the field of sociolinguistics;
- Creation of various corpora (both spoken and written);
- Speech and text processing tools for under-resourced languages and dialect variants;
- Phonology study with machine learning tools.

This year we have introduced the Special Track of Indigenous languages of Thaïland and South-East Asia in connection with co-location with ACL in Bangkok, Thailand.

We are incredibly grateful to the Field Matters program committee, who worked on peer review to give meaningful comments for each submission and made this workshop possible. We want to thank the invited speakers, Emily Prud'hommeaux, Genta Indra Winata, and Alham Fikri Aji, for contributing to the program. We would also like to mention all the authors who submitted their papers to our workshop, and we hope to continue to serve as a link between NLP specialists and field linguists.

Organizing Committee

General Chairs

Oleg Serikov, King Abdullah University of Science and Technology (KAUST)
Ekaterina Voloshina, University of Gothenburg, Chalmers University of Technology
Anna Postnikova
Saliha Muradoğlu, The Australian National University (ANU)
Eric Le Ferrand, Boston College
Elena Klyachko
Ekaterina Vylomova, University of Melbourne
Tatiana Shavrina, Meta
Francis Tyers, Indiana University

Program Committee

Program Committee

I Wayan Arka, Australian National University
Timofey Arkhangelskiy, Universität Hamburg
Alexandre Arkhipov, Universität Hamburg and Lomonosov Moscow State University
James Bednall, Charles Darwin University
Anton Buzanov, HSE University
Shobhana Lakshmi Chelliah, Indiana University at Bloomington
Michael Daniel, Collegium de Lyon
Don Daniels, University of Oregon
Kilian Evang, Heinrich Heine University Düsseldorf
Junior Pierre Eden Fevrier, University at Buffalo
Konstantin V. Filatov, HSE University
James Gray, The Australian National University (ANU)
Harald Hammarström, Uppsala University
Huade Huang, The Australian National University (ANU)
Elena Klyachko
Ezequiel Koile, Max Planck Institute for the Science of Human History
Zoey Liu, University of Florida
Tessa Masis, University of Massachusetts at Amherst
Vladislav Mikhailov, University of Oslo
David R Mortensen, Carnegie Mellon University
Saliha Muradoglu, The Australian National University (ANU)
Bruno Olsson, Universität Regensburg
Michael Proctor, Macquarie University
Emily Prud'hommeaux, Boston College
Oleg Serikov, King Abdullah University of Science and Technology
Tatiana Shavrina, Meta
Nick Thieberger, University of Melbourne
José Carlos Antonio Pérez Vargas, University at Buffalo
Albert Ventayol-Boada, University of California, Santa Barbara
Ekaterina Voloshina, Göteborg University and Chalmers University of Technology
Sasha Wilmoth, University of Melbourne
He Zhou, The Hong Kong Polytechnic University

Table of Contents

Program

Friday, August 16, 2024

09:00 - 09:30 *Opening word*

09:30 - 10:30 *Invited talk. Emily Prud'hommeaux*

10:30 - 11:00 *Coffee break*

11:00 - 11:10 *Introduction to Special Track: Indigenous languages of Thailand and South-East Asia*

11:10 - 12:10 *Talks*

Leveraging Deep Learning to Shed Light on Tones of an Endangered Language: A Case Study of Moklen
Sireemas Maspong, Francesco Burroni, Teerawee Sukanchanon, Warunsiri Pornpottanamas and Pittayawat Pittayaporn

Documenting Endangered Languages with LangDoc: A Wordlist-Based System and A Case Study on Moklen
Piyapath T Spencer

Zero-shot Cross-lingual POS Tagging for Filipino
Jimson Paulo Layacan, Isaiah Edri W. Flores, Katrina Bernice M. Tan, Ma. Regina E. Estuar, Jann Railey Montalan and Marlene M. De Leon

12:10 - 12:20 *Break*

12:20 - 13:20 *Invited talk. Genta Winata and Alham Fikri Aji*

13:20 - 13:30 *Break*

13:30 - 15:30 *Talks*

The Parallel Corpus of Russian and Ruska Romani Languages
Kirill Koncha, Abina Abina, Kazakova Tatiana and Gloria Rozovskaya

ManWav: The First Manchu ASR Model
Jean Seo, Minha Kang, SungJoo Byun and Sangah Lee

Friday, August 16, 2024 (continued)

	User-Centered Design of Digital Tools for Sociolinguistic Studies in Under-Resourced Languages Jonas Adler, Carsten Scholle, Daniel Buschek, Nicolo' Brandizzi and Muhadj Adnan
	A Comparative Analysis of Speaker Diarization Models: Creating a Dataset for German Dialectal Speech Lea Fischbach
	Noise Be Gone: Does Speech Enhancement Distort Linguistic Nuances? Iñigo Parra
	Comparing Kaldi-Based Pipeline Elpis and Whisper for Čakavian Transcription Austin Jones, Shulin Zhang, John T. Hale, Margaret Renwick, Zvjezdana Vrzic and Keith Langston
15:30 - 16:00	*Coffee break*
16:00 - 17:30	*Plenar discussion*

The Parallel Corpus of Russian and Ruska Romani Languages

Kirill Koncha[1,2*], **Abina Kukanova**[3], **Tatiana Kazakova**[3], **Gloria Rozovskaya**[3]
[1]University of Groningen, [2]Ghent University, [3]HSE University

Abstract

The paper presents a parallel corpus for the Ruska Romani dialect and Russian language. Ruska Romani is the dialect of Romani language attributed to Ruska Roma, the largest subgroup of Romani people in Russia. The corpus contains translations of Russian literature into Ruska Romani dialect. The corpus creation involved manual alignment of a small part of translations with original works, fine-tuning a language model on the aligned pairs, and using the fine-tuned model to align the remaining data. Ruska Romani sentences were annotated using a morphological analyzer, with rules crafted for proper nouns and borrowings. The corpus is available in JSON and Russian National Corpus XML formats. It includes 88,742 Russian tokens and 84,635 Ruska Romani tokens, 74,291 of which were grammatically annotated. The corpus could be used for linguistic research, including comparative and diachronic studies, bilingual dictionary creation, stylometry research, and NLP/MT tool development for Ruska Romani.

1 Introduction

Ruska Romani is the dialect of Romani language attributed to Ruska Roma, the largest subgroup of Romani people in Russia. Ruska Roma makes up at least 50% of all Romani people in Russia and the number of speakers of the dialect can be estimated at 70-90 thousand (Kozhanov, 2018).

In general, the Ruska Romani dialect is characterized by a significant influence on the Russian language at all levels It also contains a significant number of lexical grammatical borrowings from German, and Polish (Kozhanov, 2018). The Cyrillic script for the Ruska Romani dialect was developed by Dudarova and Pankov (1928).

This paper presents the parallel corpus for Ruska Romani and Russian languages. To create the corpus, we found Russian literature translated into Ruska Romani in the 1920-30s. We choose Russian literature of that period as a large number of Russian texts were translated then into minority languages as a part of government language policy (Gurbanova and Rangsikul, 2018). As a result, many of Ruska Romani written texts were created. Even today these texts make up the majority of literature written in Ruska Romani. Moreover, many of them are available in the machine-readable format. The translated texts include both fiction and non-fiction domains. We manually aligned a subsample of sentences from the translations with sentences from the original works and fine-tuned LaBSE model (Feng et al., 2022) on the aligned pairs and used it within *lingtrain-aligner* library[1] for Python to align the rest of the data. Finally, Ruska Romani sentences were annotated using *uniparser-soviet-romani*[2] library and our manually crafted rules.

The parallel corpus of Russian and Ruska Romani is available as the part Russian National Corpus (RNC)[3]. The data both in JSON format and XML format of the RNC together with code are also publicly available via our repository[4]. The corpus includes 88,742 Russian tokens and 84,635 Ruska Romani tokens, 74,291 of which are grammatically annotated.

Our parallel corpus could be used for:

- Comparative studies of Russian and Ruska Romani;
- Diachronic studies of vocabulary and grammar of Ruska Romani;
- Creation of bilingual dictionaries and study materials for Ruska Romani;

*Work is partially done while at HSE University.

[1]https://github.com/averkij/lingtrain-aligner
[2]https://github.com/burushona/uniparser-soviet-romani
[3]https://ruscorpora.ru
[4]https://github.com/kirillkoncha/ruska_romani

Proceedings of the 3rd Workshop on NLP Applications to Field Linguistics (Field Matters 2024), pages 1–5
August 16, 2024 ©2024 Association for Computational Linguistics

- Stylometry studies, investigating the influence of a translator on authorship attribution;
- Creation of NLP and MT tools for Ruska Romani.

Moreover, it contributes to the representation Ruska Romani dialect and Romani culture overall.

2 Resources for Ruska Romani

The Ruska Romani dialect is one of the most described Romani dialects. It was described in grammars by Shapoval (2007); Ventcel' (1964) and has several dictionaries created by Sergievskij and Barannikov (1938); Demeter-Charskaya (2007); Vasilevskij (2013).

However, there are almost no electronic resources for Ruska Romani dialect. The only exceptions are Romani Corpus[5] and digitized version of Russian — Ruska Romani dictionary from Shapoval (2007)[6]. The Romani Corpus contains Ruska Romani texts published in the USSR in the 1920s and 1930s (both original works and translations from Russian). The corpus consists of 720K tokens. The morphological annotations of the tokens in the corpus were not disambiguated.

Despite a large number of translations from Russian to Ruska Romani, there are no parallel corpora for these two languages.

3 Corpus Generation

3.1 Data

To create the corpus, we used Russian texts and their translations to Ruska Romani created in the 1920s and 1930s[7]. Both original texts and their translations are written in Cyrillic script. All the text sources and their metadata are presented in Table 1. The texts we used for creation of the corpus partially overlap with texts in The Romani Corpus. However, The Romani Corpus does not contain aligned sentence equivalents in Russian.

3.2 Sentence Alignment

Methods. Sentence alignment is the task of matching up equivalent sentences within the same texts in different languages. Hunalign (Varga et al., 2007) is one of the most popular tools for sentence alignment. It uses statistical models and heuristics to identify corresponding sentences based on similarity measures, such as word order and context. Another solution for this task is Vecalign (Thompson and Koehn, 2019), which employs vector space models to align sentences in a parallel corpus.

Lingtrain-aligner. We used the *lingtrain-aligner* library for the alignment task, an approach that combines both sentence embedding similarities and heuristics. Firstly, *lingtrain-aligner* selects sentence pairs with the closest vector similarity obtained from a multilingual model from an unaligned text. Then, it computes the *chain score*, a metric that estimates how well sentence indexes align with each other based on the number of breaks or discontinuities in ordered sentence pairs. The metric will be equal to *0* if all pairs are selected randomly and equal to *1* if a single line without breaks is obtained. Finally, *lingtrain-aligner* automatically resolves conflicts (cases of breaks or discontinuities) by splitting or combining sentences from one sequence.

Model for Ruska Romani. However, a language model that is trained in both languages is needed to use the *lingtrain-aligner* library. As there was no model for Ruska Romani, we trained the LaBSE model (Feng et al., 2022)[8] on Russian and Ruska Romani sentence pairs using *chain score* as an evaluation metric. The chain score was aggregated over multiple batches of ordered sentence pairs (i.e., sentences were given as they appear in original texts) several times during each epoch.

Training Set. To train the model, we used sentence pairs from randomly selected titles: *Dubrovskij*, *Malen'kie rasskazy*, *Tri medvedya*, *Posle bala*. We matched each original sentence with a translated sentence by their indexes. Then, the linguist annotator manually checked and corrected matches using Ruska Romani grammar and dictionary from Shapoval (2007). If two sentences in one language corresponded to one sentence in another language, the annotator merged these sentences into one line. The cases, when a sentence in one language did not correspond to any in another language were allowed (but were not used during training). The following texts were aligned for model training: *Dubrovskij*, *Malen'kie rasskazy*, *Tri medvedya*, *Posle bala*. In total, these texts contain 24,700 Russian tokens and 25,170 Ruska Romani tokens.

[5] `http://web-corpora.net/RomaniCorpus`

[6] `https://romadict.linghub.ru`

[7] We express our gratitude to Kirill Kozhanov for sharing the machine-readable texts from Romani Corpus.

[8] `https://huggingface.co/sentence-transformers/LaBSE`

Russian Title	English Title	Domain	Original Author	Year	№. Tokens Russian	Romani Title	Transl. Author	Transl. Year	№. Tokens Romani
Dubrovskij	Dubrovsky	Fiction	A. S. Pushkin	1833	19,249	Dubrovsko	A. Svetlovo	1936	19,957
Posle bala	After the Ball	Fiction	L. N. Tolstoy	1903	3,103	Koli progyya balo	N. Pankovo	1936	2,764
Tri medvedya	Three Bears	Fiction		1875	493	Trin rychya		1937	497
Spat' hochetsya	Sleepy	Fiction	A. P. Checkhov	1888	1,584	Te soves kamelpe	A. Svetlovo	1934	1,552
Van'ka	Vanka	Fiction		1886	1,157	Van'ka		1934	1,241
Malen'kie rasskazy	A Small Stories	Fiction	A. S. Neverov	1922	1,855	Rakiribena vash tykne chyavorenge	G. Lebedevo	1930	1,952
V brigade proryv	There's a Breakthrough in the Brigade	Fiction	M. A. Sholokhov	1930	5,126	Dre brigada proriskiribe	O. Pankovo	1934	5,299
Esli vrag ne sdayotsya, – ego unichtozhayut	If The Enemy Does Not Surrender, He is to Be Destroyed	Publicism		1930	815	Koli vrago na zdelape les has'kirna	M. Bezlyudskij	1930	583
Strasti-mordasti	Fat-Faced Passion	Fiction		1913	4,069	Strasti-mordasti		1934	4,299
Druzhki	Buddies	Fiction		1898	3,819	Druzhke		1934	3,200
Zlodei	Villains	Fiction	A. M. Gor'kij	1901	6,390	Zlodei		1934	6,038
Mal'va	Malva	Fiction		1897	12,146	Mal'va		1934	12,979
Rozhdenie cheloveka	The Birth of a Man	Fiction		1898	2,758	Manusheskiro biyanype	A. Svetlovo	1935	2,358
Na plotah	On Rafts	Fiction		1895	3,409	Pro ploty		1936	3,379
Tovarishchi	Comrades	Fiction		1895	3,845	Tovarishshi		1937	3,519
Makar Chudra	Makar Chudra	Fiction		1892	6,062	Makar Chudra		1932	3,900
Emel'yan Pilyaj	Emelyan Pilyay	Fiction		1893	3,550	Emel'yano Pilyaj		1932	2,829
K rabochim i krest'yanam	To Workers and Peasants	Publicism		1930	1,159	Ko butyar'ya	M. Bezlyudskij	1930	1,102
Son Makara	Makar's Dream	Fiction	V. G. Korolenko	1885	7,613	Makaroskiro soibe	A. Svetlovo	1935	7,187
Total					88,742				84,635

Table 1: Texts Sources

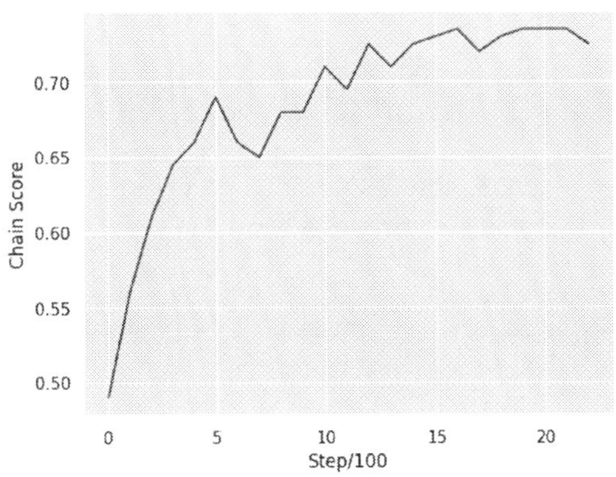

Figure 1: *Chain score* values during model training.

Training Model. The model was trained on *7* epochs or *2100* steps (each epoch had 300 steps) with batch size *6*. The evaluation was performed every *100* steps. The best *chain score* equal to *0.74* was achieved at *200* step of *5* epoch (*1600* step). The observed evaluation metrics during training are presented in Figure 1.

We used the best-trained model with *lingtrain-aligner* to automatically align the rest of the texts and resolve conflicts.

Errors Correction. Additionally, cosine similarities of each sentence pair were computed. Sentence pairs with cosine similarity below 0.5 were checked by the linguist annotator if necessary manually corrected the same way the training set was aligned. Overall, 881 sentence pairs out of 8,127 (11%) were assessed.

3.3 Morphological Annotation

For morphological annotation, we used the *uniparser-soviet-romani* library. It is a morphological analyser for Ruska Romani created based on *uniparser-morph*[9], a parser developed primarily for under-resourced languages. The parser for Ruska Romani does not perform disambiguation of analyses. Therefore, all possible annotations are given for each token. Annotations include lemma and its translation, part of speech, case, person, gender, tense, and many other features. Frequently, *unipaser-soviet-romani* dictionaries do not contain entries for loanwords from Russian or proper nouns. In total, only 84% (71,287) of tokens were annotated.

In cases where the *uniparser-soviet-romani* library did not provide the annotation, we implemented a multi-step approach to analyse nouns and proper names. Firstly, we examined whether a word has a Ruska Romani suffix. Subsequently, we removed the Ruska Romani suffix from the word. Then, we checked the word presence in Russian and its grammatical properties using *PyMorphy2* (Korobov, 2015). The final annotation process took into account both the grammatical properties of the Russian word and the grammatical properties associated with Ruska Romani suffixes. These rules allowed us to increase the amount of annotated tokens by 4% or 3,004 tokens (Figure 2).

After annotation, we converted each *uniparser-soviet-romani* word tag into RNC format. Explanations of each tag are given in the project repository (see the link above).

We did not annotate original sentences as RNC uses its tools to annotate texts in Russian (see Lyashevskaya et al. 2023; Savchuk et al. 2024).

[9]https://github.com/timarkh/uniparser-morph

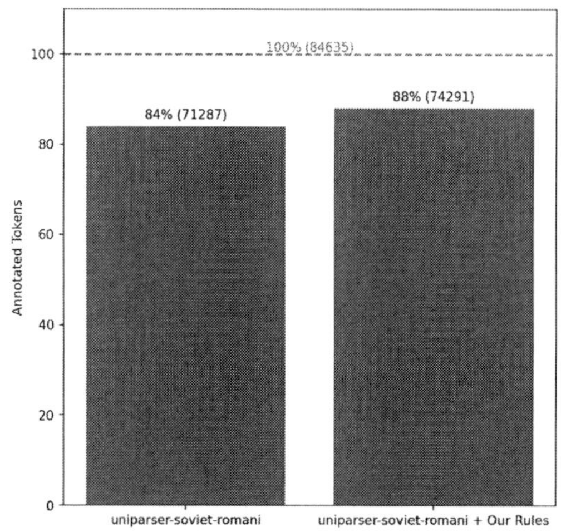

Figure 2: Annotated tokens without and with our annotation rules.

4 Data Format

Our parallel corpus is available in two formats: JSON and RNC XML. See the project repository for a more detailed description.

4.1 JSON Format

JSON annotations consist of the following fields:

- **sentence_rus**: sentence in Russian;
- **sentence_roma**: sentence in Ruska Romani;
- **sentence_id**: id of a sentence;
- **words_roma**: annotations of each Ruska Romani token in a sentence.

The first two fields are strings, the third field is numeral, and the field *words_roma* is a nested list. Each item in **words_roma** is a list of dictionaries with all possible annotations of a corresponding word in a sentence. For example, the first list in the field will contain all possible annotations of the first word in a sentence.

The annotation dictionary has the following fields:

- **wf**: word form;
- **lemma**: normalised form of a word;
- **gramm**: grammatical features of a word, such as part of speech, gender, case, etc;
- **wfGlossed**: word form divided into morphological elements by hyphens;
- **trans_en**: English translation of a word;
- **trans**: Russian translation of a word.

4.2 Russian National Corpus XML-format

We automatically converted JSON data into the XML format of RNC. The XML body consists of the following containers:

- **<para>**: container for a sentence pair, includes attributes **id** and **id_str**;
- **<se>**: container for a sentence within a sentence pair, includes attribute **lang** that could either be **rus** for Russian or **rom** for Ruska Romani;
- **<w>**: container for a word level annotation, applied only to sentences in Ruska Romani;
- **<ana>**: container inside **<w>** that stores grammatical features of a word.

The **<ana>** container has following attributes:

- **lex**: lemma of a word;
- **wordf**: word form;
- **gr**: grammatical features of a word;
- **transl**: Russian translation of a word.

  One word container **<w>** could include several annotation containers **<ana>**.

5 Conclusion

We presented the parallel corpus for Russian and Ruska Romani languages. For sentence alignment, we used a model trained on manually aligned sentences. We also manually checked alignment in sentence pairs, where the model predicted low similarity for sentences. Ruska Romani sentences in the corpus were annotated using *uniparser-soviet-romani* library and our own manually crafted rules. The data is available in JSON and RNC XML formats.

Our work could be used in different areas: from linguistic research and language teaching to the creation of NLP tools and resources for Ruska Romani. It also contributes to the representation of Ruska Romani dialect and Romani culture as the corpus is available in RNC, one of the largest platforms with resources for the Russian language and minority languages of Russia.

Limitations

The present work has several limitations. The first limitation is the absence of disambiguation in morphological annotation. Secondly, in the case of Russian sentence annotation, we rely on RNC annotation tools which are not publicly available. Finally, the corpus includes only translations of Russian literature and does not include any spoken language. Moreover, the texts were translated a long time ago and might not fully reflect the current state of the Ruska Romani dialect.

Acknowledgments

We express gratitude to Kirill Kozhanov for sharing texts in Ruska Romani; to Timofey Arhangel'skij for creating *uniparser-soviet-romani*; to Dmitry Sitchinava for help with data conversion to RNC format; to Olga Lyahevskaya, Svetlana Toldova, Denis Pisarenko, and Maxim Bazhukov for valuable feedback; to Fedor Samodov for help with manual sentence alignment.

References

O.S. Demeter-Charskaya. 2007. *Cygansko-russkij i russko-cyganskij slovar' (dialekt russkih cygan)*. Moskva.

N. A. Dudarova and N. A. Pankov. 1928. *Nevo drom. Bukvare vash bare manushenge*. Moscow.

Fangxiaoyu Feng, Yinfei Yang, Daniel Cer, Naveen Arivazhagan, and Wei Wang. 2022. Language-agnostic BERT sentence embedding. In *Proceedings of the 60th Annual Meeting of the Association for Computational Linguistics (Volume 1: Long Papers)*, pages 878–891, Dublin, Ireland. Association for Computational Linguistics.

Nubar Gurbanova and Rungthum Rangsikul. 2018. Language in politics features of the soviet language policy in 1920s-1930s. In *Proceedings of the International Conference on Language Phenomena in Multimodal Communication (KLUA 2018)*, pages 418–422. Atlantis Press.

Mikhail Korobov. 2015. Morphological analyzer and generator for Russian and Ukrainian languages. In Mikhail Yu. Khachay, Natalia Konstantinova, Alexander Panchenko, Dmitry I. Ignatov, and Valeri G. Labunets, editors, *Analysis of Images, Social Networks and Texts*, volume 542 of *Communications in Computer and Information Science*, pages 320–332. Springer International Publishing.

Kirill Kozhanov. 2018. Cyganskij yazyk i ego dialekty. In N.G. Demeter and A.V. Chernyh, editors, *Cygane*, Narody i kul'tury, pages 156–159. Nauka, Moscow, Russia.

Olga Lyashevskaya, Ivan Afanasev, Sergey Rebrikov, Yulia Shishkina, Elvira Suleymanova, Ivan Trofimov, and Natalia Vlasova. 2023. Disambiguation in context in the russian national corpus: 20 years later. In *Computational Linguistics and Intellectual Technologies: Papers from the Annual International Conf. "Dialogue"*, volume 22, pages 307–318.

S. O. Savchuk, T. A. Arhangel'skij, A. A. Bonch-Osmolovskaya, O. V. Donina, YU. N. Kuznecova, O. N. Lyashevskaya, B. V. Orekhov, and M. V. Podryadchikova. 2024. Nacional'nyj korpus russkogo yazyka 2.0: novye vozmozhnosti i perspektivy razvitiya. *Voprosy yazykoznaniya*, 2:7–34.

M.V Sergievskij and A.P. Barannikov. 1938. *Cygansko-russkij slovar': Okolo 10000 slov s prilozheniem grammatiki cyganskogo yazyka*. Moskva.

V.V. Shapoval. 2007. *Samouchitel' cyganskogo yazyka*. Moskva.

Brian Thompson and Philipp Koehn. 2019. Vecalign: Improved sentence alignment in linear time and space. In *Proceedings of the 2019 Conference on Empirical Methods in Natural Language Processing and the 9th International Joint Conference on Natural Language Processing (EMNLP-IJCNLP)*, pages 1342–1348, Hong Kong, China. Association for Computational Linguistics.

Dávid Varga, Péter Halácsy, András Kornai, Nagy Viktor, László Nagy, Lajos Németh, and Viktor Trón. 2007. Parallel corpora for medium density languages. In *Amsterdam Studies in the Theory and History of Linguistic Science. Series 4, Current Issues in Linguistic Theory*, pages 247–258.

N.A. Vasilevskij. 2013. *Romany chib: Cygansko-russkij slovar'*. Kaliningrad.

T.V. Ventcel'. 1964. *Cyganskij yazyk (severnorusskij dialekt)*. Moskva.

ManWav: The First Manchu ASR Model

Jean Seo, Minha Kang, Sungjoo Byun, Sangah Lee
Seoul National University
{seemdog, alsgk1123, byunsj, sanalee}@snu.ac.kr

Abstract

This study addresses the widening gap in Automatic Speech Recognition (ASR) research between high resource and extremely low resource languages, with a particular focus on Manchu, a critically endangered language. Manchu exemplifies the challenges faced by marginalized linguistic communities in accessing state-of-the-art technologies. In a pioneering effort, we introduce the first-ever Manchu ASR model *ManWav*, leveraging Wav2Vec2-XLSR-53. The results of the first Manchu ASR is promising, especially when trained with our augmented data. Wav2Vec2-XLSR-53 fine-tuned with augmented data demonstrates a 0.02 drop in CER and 0.13 drop in WER compared to the same base model fine-tuned with original data.

1 Introduction

The landscape of Automatic Speech Recognition (ASR) research has centered around high resource languages such as English. This concentrated attention on high resource languages has deepened the divide between research advancements. While research on English ASR encompasses diverse linguistic variations, including accented and noised speech, the same cannot be said for many low resource languages, though a few basic research including Safonova et al. (2022) and Zhou et al. (2022) exist. Astonishingly, not a single basic ASR model has been developed for Manchu to date, highlighting a critical void in linguistic inclusivity within the realm of ASR technology.

The development of a Manchu ASR model holds particular importance in the field of linguistics, as there are no more native speakers of Manchu. Consequently, the available data, whether text or audio, for linguistic study is limited and cannot be replenished. Therefore, it is crucial to maximize the utilization of existing data. However, due to the scarcity of individuals capable of transcribing Manchu audio data, unlabeled data remain unused. If transcribed, this data could prove to be invaluable resource for Manchu research and preservation. Even though the performance of the Manchu ASR system may not be perfect, it would be immensely helpful if it could provide draft transcriptions. This would enable researchers to revise and incorporate them into their studies.

This paper sets out to address the significant gap between high and low resource languages by developing the inaugural Manchu ASR model. This endeavor is underscored by the scarcity of linguistic resources, prompting us to collect all existing Manchu audio data from Kim et al. (2008) in one channel. We try to maximize the cross-lingual capabilities of Wav2Vec2-XLSR-53 (Conneau et al., 2020) by fine-tuning the model with Manchu audio data. The performance of the Manchu ASR model is further enhanced through data augmentation.

The contributions of this study are as follows:

- Collecting Manchu audio data in an unified format and correcting corresponding transcriptions
- Developing the very first Manchu ASR model with augmented data

2 Manchu Language

The Manchu language, a member of the Tungusic linguistic family, has its roots among the Manchu people of Northeast China and boasts a significant historical role as the official language of the Qing dynasty (1644-1912). Presently, the language confronts a dire state of endangerment, officially denoted a dead language with no more native speakers left.

There have been some efforts to employ technological solutions in the preservation and revitalization of Manchu. These endeavors include the Manchu spell checker (You, 2014), Manchu-Korean machine translation (Seo et al., 2023), and

Proceedings of the 3rd Workshop on NLP Applications to Field Linguistics (Field Matters 2024), pages 6–11
August 16, 2024 ©2024 Association for Computational Linguistics

Manchu NER/POS tagging models (Lee et al., 2024). However, due to the paucity of data, the studies above face challenges and no ASR model has been yet developed.

3 Data

3.1 Materials

This study leverages Colloquial Manchu data provided by Kim et al. (2008), in which Colloquial Manchu data is gathered as part of ASK REAL project (Altaic Society of Korea, Researches on Endangered Altaic Languagess (Choi et al., 2012)). This audio data represents the dialect of Sanjiazi village, located in the Youyi Dowoerzu Manzu Ke'er-kezizu township, Fuyu county, Heilongjiang Province.

The recording took place from February 7th to 14th, 2006 in Qiqihar, Heilongjiang Province, with Mr. Meng Xianxiao (73 years old at that moment). Though Chinese being his first language, Mr. Meng Xianxiao sufficiently served as the speaker, acquiring a comprehensive ability of Manchu by the age of 12.

The data we use in this study is the recordings of the basic conversational expressions and the sentences for grammatical analysis. The length of each recording is 32 minutes and 58 minutes, for a total of 90 minutes. Corresponding transcriptions are basically provided by Kim et al. (2008) and went through some revisions by a Manchu researcher from Seoul National University for better precision.

3.2 Transcription

The phoneme transcription system in this study is based on Kim et al. (2008). While it shares similarities with the International Phonetic Alphabet (IPA), our system incorporates some distinctions. Specifically, /b, d, g/ represent voiceless unaspirated stops, and /p, t, k/ denote voiceless aspirated stops. Notably, Colloquial Manchu lacks voiced stops, making this transcription system more practical than using diacritic /ʰ/ to indicate aspiration. Next, /ǰ, č, š/ denote voiceless palatal sounds. In IPA system, corresponding sound symbols are [ɟ, ç, ɕ]. But /ǰ/ is not voiced unlike [ɟ], and /č/ is the aspirated sound, [čʰ]. Some examples can be found in Table 1.

Transcription	IPA
miŋ ənjə bitk səwə.	miŋ əniə pitk səwə.
(Translation: My mother is a teacher.)	
došən ǰo.	toʐ̺ən dʐ̺o.
(Translation: Come on in.)	

Table 1: Examples of our transcription, IPA, and corresponding translation.

3.3 Data Augmentation

The scarcity of speech datasets from native Manchu speakers presents a significant challenge, necessitating the adoption of various data augmentation methods. Audio data augmentation methods used to simulate different acoustic environments include:

- **Additive noise**: Adding background noise to the audio samples.
- **Clipping**: Involves cutting short the audio signals.
- **Reverberation**: Applying reverberation effects.
- **Time dropout**: Randomly removing segments of the audio.

By implementing the above techniques through WavAugment[1] provided by Kharitonov et al. (2020), we expand the dataset by 100% respectively, to a total of 400%, significantly enriching the available train data. Notable is the fact that data augmentation is implemented after the separation of train and test data, ensuring more reliable test results by preventing overlap between the train and test sets. The size of data before and after augmentation is described in Table 2.

Before Augmentation	Duration
train	81 min
test	9.5 min
After Augmentation	**Duration**
train	326.5 min
test	9.5 min

Table 2: The duration of audio files(.wav) in minutes before and after augmentation.

[1]https://github.com/facebookresearch/WavAugment

4 Experiment

4.1 Models

Wav2Vec2-XLSR-53 (Conneau et al., 2020) is utilized as the base model. Wav2Vec2-XLSR-53 is a multilingual self-supervised learning (SSL) model from Meta AI[2] pre-trained with 53 languages. A Wav2Vec2-XLSR-53 model is fine-tuned in two different types of data, leading to two separate fine-tuned models: one with original Manchu data, and the other with augmented Manchu data. We name the model trained with augmented data *ManWav*. The fine-tuning process is conducted through HuggingSound (Grosman, 2022).

4.2 Experimental Setup

Our experiments are conducted using an NVIDIA A100 GPU. We fine-tune our models with learning rate 3e-4, batch size 16, and dropout rate of 0.1. We train Wav2Vec2-XLSR-53 with 400% augmented data for 1 epoch. On the other hand, Wav2Vec2-XLSR-53 with original data is trained for 5 epochs, ensuring identical train data size for fair comparison.

5 Result and Discussion

5.1 Result

We use Character Error Rate (CER) and Word Error Rate (WER) as evaluation metrics. CER assesses the accuracy of character transcription, while WER measures the correctness of word recognition. Scores closer to 0 represent better performances in both metrics. WER and CER are the most common and essential metrics in gauging the overall performance of ASR systems.

The experimental results prove the significance of data augmentation in fine-tuning the base model. As depicted in Table 3, using augmented data at the training stage clearly improves the performance, specifically dropping CER by 0.02 and WER by 0.13, indicating the effectiveness using augmented data described in Section 3.3.

Moreover, Table 4 shows the promising capabilities of *ManWav* in the Manchu speech recognition task. The achieved accuracy is particularly noteworthy given the limited availability of Manchu speech data and considering that Wav2Vec2-XLSR-53 is not initially pre-trained on Manchu.

[2]https://ai.meta.com/

Data Augmentation	CER	WER
before	0.13	0.44
after	**0.11**	**0.31**

Table 3: The performance of Wav2Vec2-XLSR-53 each trained with data before and after augmentation.

5.2 Linguistic Analysis

Taking into account the linguistic characteristics of Manchu, we classify the most common errors in *ManWav* into the following four categories: (1) confusion involving /ə/, (2) confusion and nasalizing of nasal sounds in word-final positions, (3) assimilation between stops, and (4) confusion between /w/ and /x/.

First, there are some uncaptured or mismatched /ə/ sounds in the inference results, particularly in word-final or between sonorants (e.g., /l/) and stops. This occurs because /ə/ can be neutralized with other vowels or even deleted, posing challenges in accurate transcription. As shown in table 4, the locative marker *de* and *amə* 'dad' are sometimes captured as *d* and *am*, indicating apocope of /ə/. The loss of /ə/ is also evident in *dulke*, which originally included /ə/ between the sonorant /l/ and the stop /k/.

Moreover, nasal sounds /n/ and /m/ in word-final positions are frequently overlooked during inference. This could be attributed to the nature of nasal sounds, as they tend to be fused with subsequent vowels, resulting in nasalized vowels, or they may be omitted altogether. The word *gunin* 'thought' is an instance of this phenomenon. It is often transcribed as *gunim*, where the final /n/ appears as /m/. The occurrence of nasal stops can sometimes be mistaken for the deletion of the nasalized preceding vowel. For example, the /n/ sound in *ilan* 'three' typically nasalizes the following vowels and then is deleted. However, our model erroneously retained the nasal sound in the transcription *ilan*, preserving the final /n/.

Third, the inference results contain pairs that have undergone assimilation based on the articulated position. These pairs were not transcribed as assimilated forms, but this kind of assimilation is a highly productive phenomenon in natural languages. For instance, the /mg/ sequence in *damgu* 'tobacco' became /ŋg/ in our inference results. This is unsurprising since both /ŋ/ and /g/ are velar whereas /m/ is bilabial.

Lastly, confusion between intervocalic /w/ and

Model Prediction	Actual Transcription
si jawuči bi gəl jaam si jawuči bi gəl jaam	si jawuči bi gəl jaam si jawuči bi gəl jaam
tələ am dulkə ani əmkə iči bo aləxə	tələ amə duləkə ani əmkə iči bo aləxə
bi sajwə wakə bi sajwə wakə	bi sajwə wakə bi sajwə wakə
bi siskə bitk xolal ba də jom mutulko	bi siskə bitk xolal ba də jom mutulko
min do bitk xolal ba joxo	min do bitk xolal ba joxo
odun gjak šaxulo odun gjak šaxulo	odun gjak šawulo odun gjak šawulo

Table 4: Examples of inference results from *ManWav*. Wrong predictions are marked red and the corresponding answers are marked blue.

/x/ is frequently observed. To be specific, *šawulo* 'cold' is recognized as *šaxulo* in our model. Given that /w/ is the labial approximant and /x/ is the palatal approximant, it can be noted that these two sounds occupy distinct articulatory positions. However, there is no equivalent unvoiced sound for /w/, and discerning the voicing of approximants becomes challenging when they are in intervocalic positions.

The above four types of mismatch and corresponding examples are elaborated in Table 5.

Mismatch Types	Examples
(1) ə / __#, R__C	də : d, amə : am, duləkə : dulkə
(2) n, m / __#	gunin : gunim, ilan : ila
(3) assimilation	damgu : daŋgu
(4) w : x / V__V	šaxulo : šawulo

Table 5: Observed mismatch examples from the inference results written in phonological notations. R refers to sonorants, C consonants, and V vowels. # means boundary of words; __# means word-final position.

6 Related Work

6.1 ASR research in low-resource languages

There exist some endeavors to apply ASR to low-resource languages. For example, Safonova et al. (2022) collect a speech dataset in the Chukchi language and train an XLSR model. Similarly, Qin et al. (2022) improve low-resource Tibetan ASR while Jimerson and Prud'hommeaux (2018) introduce a fully functional ASR system tailored for Seneca, an endangered indigenous language of North America. Singh et al. (2023) propose an effective self-training approach capable of generating accurate pseudo-labels for unlabeled low-resource speech, particularly for the Punjabi language. Furthermore, Zhou et al. (2022) explore training strategies for efficient data utilization and Bartelds et al. (2023) investigate data augmentation methods to enhance ASR systems for low-resource scenarios. Other efforts for multilingual ASR or adapting to low-resource scenarios include Kaldi-toolkit[3], IARPA Babel project[4]. However, as an extremely endangered language, Manchu has been isolated from all these efforts.

6.2 Wav2Vec 2.0

The core innovation of Wav2Vec 2.0 (Baevski et al., 2020) lies in its ability to effectively capture the contextual information in speech through its Transformer-based architecture (Vaswani et al., 2023). Wav2Vec 2.0 leverages self-supervised training, allowing the training of an ASR model with a minimal amount of labeled data, provided there is an ample supply of unlabeled data. Wav2Vec 2.0 is effective not only in capturing diverse dialects but also in accommodating various languages. XLSR (Conneau et al., 2020) is built on Wav2Vec 2.0 and learns cross-lingual speech representations from raw waveform of speech in multiple languages. XLSR-53 is particularly pretrained on 53 languages, and fine-tuned for Connectionist Temporal Classification(CTC) speech recognition. CTC is a technique used in encoder-only transformer models such as Wav2Vec 2.0, HuBERT (Hsu et al., 2021) and M-CTC-T (Lugosch et al., 2022).

7 Conclusion and Future Work

As an extremely low resource language, Manchu has often been overlooked in linguistic technology. In an effort to maximize the utilization of available Manchu data, the development of an ASR system is essential. We introduce *ManWav*, which involves fine-tuning Wav2Vec2-XLSR-53 on augmented Manchu audio data, with the aim of providing a valuable tool for the study and preservation

[3]https://kaldi-asr.org/index.html

[4]https://www.iarpa.gov/research-programs/babel

of Manchu. As the addition of a decoder to an ASR model is known to boost the inference performance (Karita et al., 2019; Zeyer et al., 2019), enhancing the inference quality with the help of a language model should be studied in the future.

Limitations

The primary constraint of this research lies in the scarcity of Manchu audio data. As the audio data used in this research consists only of Colloquial Manchu from one speaker, utilizing *ManWav* in other domains would not show optimized performances, given that ASR models are usually heavily domain-dependent.

Ethics Statement

The project paves the way for further innovations in the field and emphasizes the importance of inclusivity in technological advancements, ensuring that the benefits of state-of-the-art technologies are accessible to all linguistic groups, regardless of their resource status. To support further ASR studies on endangered languages, we plan to release *ManWav* in public.

References

Alexei Baevski, Henry Zhou, Abdelrahman Mohamed, and Michael Auli. 2020. wav2vec 2.0: A framework for self-supervised learning of speech representations.

Martijn Bartelds, Nay San, Bradley McDonnell, Dan Jurafsky, and Martijn Wieling. 2023. Making more of little data: Improving low-resource automatic speech recognition using data augmentation.

Wonho Choi, Hyunjo You, and Juwon Kim. 2012. The documentation of endangered altaic languages and the creation of a digital archive to safeguard linguistic diversity. *International Journal of Intangible Heritage*, 0(7):103–111.

Alexis Conneau, Alexei Baevski, Ronan Collobert, Abdelrahman Mohamed, and Michael Auli. 2020. Unsupervised cross-lingual representation learning for speech recognition.

Jonatas Grosman. 2022. HuggingSound: A toolkit for speech-related tasks based on Hugging Face's tools. `https://github.com/jonatasgrosman/huggingsound`.

Wei-Ning Hsu, Benjamin Bolte, Yao-Hung Hubert Tsai, Kushal Lakhotia, Ruslan Salakhutdinov, and Abdelrahman Mohamed. 2021. Hubert: Self-supervised speech representation learning by masked prediction of hidden units.

Robbie Jimerson and Emily Prud'hommeaux. 2018. ASR for documenting acutely under-resourced indigenous languages. In *Proceedings of the Eleventh International Conference on Language Resources and Evaluation (LREC 2018)*, Miyazaki, Japan. European Language Resources Association (ELRA).

Shigeki Karita, Nanxin Chen, Tomoki Hayashi, Takaaki Hori, Hirofumi Inaguma, Ziyan Jiang, Masao Someki, Nelson Enrique Yalta Soplin, Ryuichi Yamamoto, Xiaofei Wang, Shinji Watanabe, Takenori Yoshimura, and Wangyou Zhang. 2019. A comparative study on transformer vs rnn in speech applications. In *2019 IEEE Automatic Speech Recognition and Understanding Workshop (ASRU)*. IEEE.

Eugene Kharitonov, Morgane Rivière, Gabriel Synnaeve, Lior Wolf, Pierre-Emmanuel Mazaré, Matthijs Douze, and Emmanuel Dupoux. 2020. Data augmenting contrastive learning of speech representations in the time domain.

Juwon Kim, Dongho Ko, Chaoke D. O., and Boldyrev B. V. Han Youfeng, Piao Lianyu. 2008. *Materials of Spoken Manchu*. Seoul National University Press.

Sangah Lee, Sungjoo Byun, Jean Seo, and Minha Kang. 2024. ManNER & ManPOS: Pioneering NLP for endangered Manchu language. In *Proceedings of the 2024 Joint International Conference on Computational Linguistics, Language Resources and Evaluation (LREC-COLING 2024)*, pages 11030–11039, Torino, Italia. ELRA and ICCL.

Loren Lugosch, Tatiana Likhomanenko, Gabriel Synnaeve, and Ronan Collobert. 2022. Pseudo-labeling for massively multilingual speech recognition.

S. Qin, L. Wang, S. Li, Longbiao Wang, Sheng Li, Jianwu Dang, and Lixin Pan. 2022. Improving low-resource tibetan end-to-end asr by multilingual and multilevel unit modeling. *EURASIP Journal on Audio, Speech, and Music Processing*, 2022.

Anastasia Safonova, Tatiana Yudina, Emil Nadimanov, and Cydnie Davenport. 2022. Automatic speech recognition of low-resource languages based on chukchi.

Jean Seo, Sungjoo Byun, Minha Kang, and Sangah Lee. 2023. Mergen: The first manchu-korean machine translation model trained on augmented data.

Satwinder Singh, Feng Hou, and Ruili Wang. 2023. A novel self-training approach for low-resource speech recognition.

Ashish Vaswani, Noam Shazeer, Niki Parmar, Jakob Uszkoreit, Llion Jones, Aidan N. Gomez, Lukasz Kaiser, and Illia Polosukhin. 2023. Attention is all you need.

Hyun-Jo You. 2014. A manchu speller: With a practical introduction to the natural language processing of minority languages. *Altai Hakpo*, 24:39–67.

Albert Zeyer, Parnia Bahar, Kazuki Irie, Ralf Schluter, and Hermann Ney. 2019. A comparison of transformer and lstm encoder decoder models for asr. *2019 IEEE Automatic Speech Recognition and Understanding Workshop (ASRU)*, pages 8–15.

Zhikai Zhou, Wei Wang, Wangyou Zhang, and Yanmin Qian. 2022. Exploring effective data utilization for low-resource speech recognition. In *ICASSP 2022 - 2022 IEEE International Conference on Acoustics, Speech and Signal Processing (ICASSP)*, pages 8192–8196.

User-Centered Design of Digital Tools for Sociolinguistic Studies in Under-Resourced Languages

Jonas Adler* and **Carsten Scholle*** and **Daniel Buschek**
University of Bayreuth, Mobile Intelligent User Interfaces
{name}.{surname}@uni-bayreuth.de

Nicolo' Brandizzi
Sapienza University of Rome, DIAG
brandizzi@uniroma1.it

Muhadj Adnan
University of Bayreuth, Arabic Studies
muhadj.adnan@uni-bayreuth.de

Abstract

Investigating language variation is a core aspect of sociolinguistics, especially through the use of linguistic corpora. Collecting and analyzing spoken language in text-based corpora can be time-consuming and error-prone, especially for under-resourced languages with limited software assistance. This paper explores the language variation research process using a User-Centered Design (UCD) approach from the field of Human-Computer Interaction (HCI), offering guidelines for the development of digital tools for sociolinguists. We interviewed four researchers, observed their workflows and software usage, and analyzed the data using Grounded Theory. This revealed key challenges in manual tasks, software assistance, and data management. Based on these insights, we identified a set of requirements that future tools should meet to be valuable for researchers in this domain. The paper concludes by proposing design concepts with sketches and prototypes based on the identified requirements. These concepts aim to guide the implementation of a fully functional, open-source tool. This work presents an interdisciplinary approach between sociolinguistics and HCI by emphasizing the practical aspects of research that are often overlooked.

1 Introduction

Researchers in sociolinguistics often use corpora for investigations of language structure and usage, identifying linguistic characteristics and patterns in different contexts. Researchers gain insights into these patterns by analyzing a collection of authentic texts (corpora) quantitatively and/or qualitatively (Biber et al., 1998). The importance of this field has particularly increased due to factors such as global interconnection and continuous increase in migration. Notably, the growing contact of speakers of different languages and varieties adds relevance to investigating and analyzing language variation and change. This research often involves collecting and transcribing natural spoken language to identify distinct linguistic features and discover patterns during analysis, though other methods, such as sociolinguistic experiments, are also employed.

Yet, the potential of this research area is frequently accompanied by many challenges that influence how research is conducted. For instance, the exponential increase of available data enhances the possibilities for research, but dealing with these large quantities of data poses new challenges for researchers and requires them to incorporate computer-assisted tools (Mair, 2018). However, transitioning to digital solutions can be difficult when faced with unfamiliar tools and a lack of knowledge about research strategies. In under-resourced languages, these issues are often compounded by the absence of assistance tools, like automatic language recognition software, leading to a time-consuming manual transcription process (Chakravarthi et al., 2019). This *transcription bottleneck* (Bird, 2021) is particularly problematic for under-resourced languages due to transcription difficulties. This raises the question of whether current research techniques can keep up with advancing technology and changing language dynamics.

In this paper, we aim to create a bridge between Human-Computer Interaction (HCI) and linguistics, fostering an interdisciplinary collaboration that leverages the strengths of both fields. By focusing on a *User-Centered Design* (UCD) approach, we investigate the practical workflows currently carried out by variationist sociolinguists working with lesser-resourced languages, using research on Arabic dialects as a case study. We aim to identify critical areas, such as data management, digital annotation, and automatic analysis, that limit the efficiency and quality of their studies. The outcomes intended to be applicable to a broader range

*These authors contributed equally to this work.

Proceedings of the 3rd Workshop on NLP Applications to Field Linguistics (Field Matters 2024), pages 12–27
August 16, 2024 ©2024 Association for Computational Linguistics

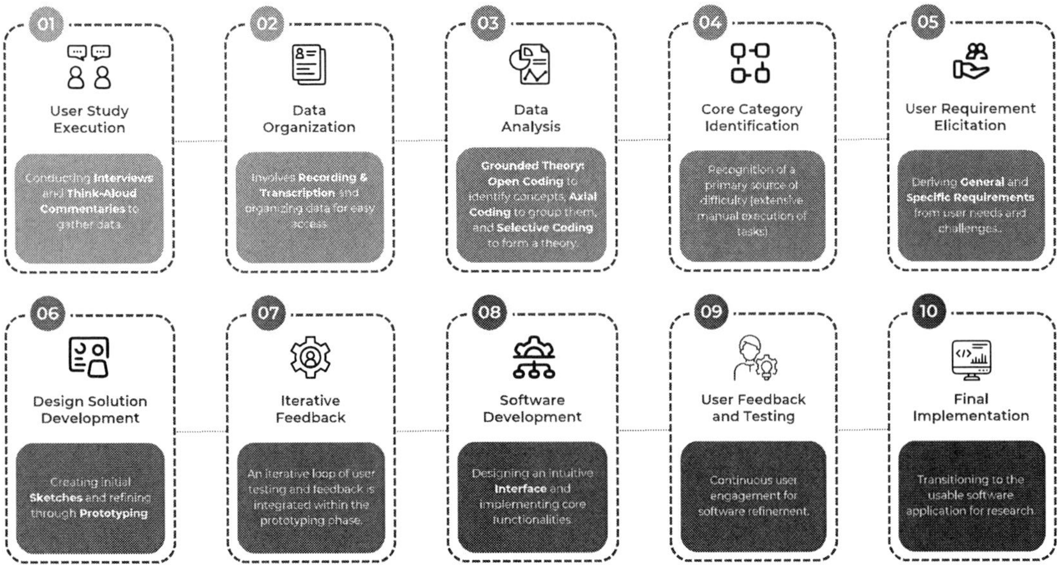

Figure 1: The *User-Centered Design Process*: steps from initial user studies and analysis to iterative design solution development, highlighting the continuous user feedback integration needed for user-friendly software interfaces.

of lesser-resourced languages. As many existing software applications invest insufficient effort in the identification of user needs for these languages, we introduce a road map for finding suitable technical solutions. Our approach enables the creation of a digital tool specifically designed to meet researchers' needs. Moreover, by actively involving researchers in the design process and valuing their feedback, we ensure that the software will be user-friendly and tailored to their requirements.

The upcoming sections outline our approach, starting with a theoretical background and overview of related works (Section 2), followed by data collection through interviews with researchers specializing in different Arabic varieties (see Section 3.1). This is followed by an in-depth data analysis (see Section 3.2 and 4.1). We then define the requirements and constraints for a user-centered software solution by considering the unique needs and challenges in this field (Section 4.2). Building on these insights, we propose a prototype that extends and enhances a previously developed tool, *CorpusCompass* (Adnan and Brandizzi, 2023), reflecting our dedication to improving the software in line with evolving research demands and user insights. Our goal is to narrow the divide between theoretical research and practical utility.

2 Theoretical Background and Related Work

This section reviews the theoretical background and relevant literature. Central to this discussion is an exploration of *User-Centered Design* principles and their various extensions (Section 2.1), which are crucial to our approach. Additionally, we present an overview of current software solutions in this domain (Section 2.5). While our work touches on language variation research, we primarily focus on UCD aspects in this section. For more detailed information on language variation research methods, please refer to Tagliamonte (2006).

2.1 User-Centered Design

User-Centered Design is the guiding principle of our research, emphasizing that software and design development should prioritize users' needs, skills, and challenges (Abras et al., 2004)(Sharp et al., 2019).

UCD proposes several key concepts and steps that can lead to a successful design process, Figure 1. One of these concepts is consulting users throughout all phases of development, especially in its early stages. This includes studying how users perform their tasks to achieve their goals, as well as understanding their preferences and characteristics. Design decisions should be informed by user research, and the process should be iterative to allow for continuous user feedback and flexible adjustments(Lowdermilk, 2013).

Advantages of UCD The primary benefit of involving users during the development process is ensuring usability for the intended software. This is achieved by tailoring the design to address the specific problems of the users. The usability of an application is a major indicator of whether the application will be relevant for practical use or not, which makes it one of the most important factors for developing any design solution (Ritter et al., 2014).

Better usability can also impact other aspects of the users' interaction with the application. Examples include greater productivity, improved user experience, or increased accessibility (de Normalización, 2010). Consistently communicating requirements and solution concepts with target users also contributes to better expectation management. Expectation management involves clearly defining the expectations users should have regarding software functionality. This prevents failing to meet user expectations, such as not fulfilling specified requirements, which could lead to resistance or rejection of software adoption (Sharp et al., 2019).

2.2 Think-Aloud Commentaries

Think-Aloud Commentaries (TaC) are a specialized form of observations often employed in user research (Nielsen, 2012). They are used to collect user feedback within a designated research setting, for example in the context of software application design and evaluation. During TaCs, participants are asked to perform a set of representative tasks while simultaneously verbalizing all of their thoughts regarding their task execution. TaCs can be used as a data collection technique that allows for capturing subtleties and details that may go unnoticed or forgotten with alternative data collection methodologies (such as interviews and workshops). Additionally, they are also flexible and require minimal resources, which allows for easy implementation across a broad spectrum of research scenarios and online settings (Cotton and Gresty, 2006).

2.3 Grounded Theory

Grounded Theory (GT) (Corbin and Strauss, 1990) is a methodology for qualitative data analysis for text-based data sources. It enables the identification of underlying concepts in the dataset and the exploration of their relations, therefore creating a deeper understanding of the data. This is achieved by the derivation of an overarching theory, that is "grounded" in the data and explains the underlying concepts. Implementing a Grounded Theory approach usually consists of three distinct steps that help with summarizing and organizing the collected data, and therefore being able to extract valuable information from it.

The first step, *open coding*, is concerned with breaking down the data from the transcripts and notes into distinct *codes*. Each *code* is a short key phrase that precisely encapsulates an identified concept in the data. The second phase, *axial coding*, aims at grouping established *codes* that are thematically similar into different categories, as well as finding relationships between these *code groups*. Lastly, *selective coding* describes the process of formulating an overarching theory that strings all identified concepts and categories together. Core categories can be selected that serve as the foundation for this theory (Corbin and Strauss, 1990).

Additionally, it should be pointed out that these steps do not necessarily imply a fixed chronological order, but can also be performed in iterations and repetitions.

2.4 Requirements and Prototyping

Requirements dictate the necessary functionalities that a product must possess to address the previously identified issues or provide assistance in task execution (Sharp et al., 2019). After gathering sufficient amounts of data to understand the users' workflows and challenges, product (in our case, software) requirements can be specified. Over the course of this paper, product requirements will be referred to as *user requirements*. This is generally a more intuitive expression for this concept, as it implies the involvement of the user.

Requirements form the foundation for the creation of prototypes, which serve as preliminary models of the intended product or software. During prototyping, alternative design solutions are developed with the objective of identifying the most fitting design for the application context. In the context of UCD, prototyping should be integrated into an iterative process with sustained user feedback, where prototypes can be improved over different cycles (see Section 2.1). It should be pointed out that shifting the focus towards the consideration of technological possibilities should occur only at this stage of the UCD process. However, these possibilities should not serve as the driving factor for development, but rather as answers on how to fulfill the identified requirements (Sharp et al., 2019).

2.5 Challenges in Existing Software

The study of language variation has attracted scholarly attention since the 1960s (Bayley, 2013). Early research, such as Labov's studies from that era (Labov, 2006), explored the direct relationships between linguistic and social variables without complex statistical methods. Initially, researchers primarily used simple quantitative techniques, such as percentages, cross-tabulations, and multivariate analysis (Walker, 2012; Guy, 2013). Over time, there has been a shift toward more sophisticated analytical methods. Moreover, technological advancements have led to the development of various software applications that facilitate quantitative research tasks within this domain. However, the majority of these tools are designed for a restricted subset of languages, thereby neglecting under-resourced languages (Mair, 2018).

In this field, one essential software requirement is the ability to annotate text corpora. Numerous software solutions have been developed to meet this need. Neves and Ševa (2019) conducted a comparative analysis of various annotation tools based on specific criteria. Among the tools evaluated, *WebAnno* (Yimam et al., 2013), *Brat* (Stenetorp et al., 2012), *FLAT*, and *EzTag* (Kwon et al., 2018) proved to be the best rated options. Nevertheless, none of the tools mentioned a user-centered approach during development. As a result, linguists often need to work within the limitations of these tools, rather than having tools that are flexible enough to meet their diverse requirements (Mair, 2018).

3 Methodology

This Section details the strategies for data collection (Section 3.1) and analysis (Section 3.2). It also describes how these results inform user requirements (Section 3.3), which are the core findings of this paper.

3.1 Data Collection

The data collection procedure included conducting open interviews with researchers studying language variation, as well as directly observing their workflows during a Think-Aloud Commentary (step 1, Figure 1). While TaCs are typically implemented for the evaluation of design solutions, in our study, they were used to gain detailed insights into the users' workflows and to identify the problem space.

In total, four academics from different universities participated in our user study. All of them are active researchers in Arabic linguistics and specialized in the study of different dialects (among less-resourced languages) based on oral speech (see Appendix B for users' specializations). None of the participants had prior experience with programming own solutions for their respective research tasks. The number of participants was chosen in accordance with the minimum required for discovering usability problems (Alroobaea and Mayhew, 2014; Zapata and Pow-Sang, 2012). The gathered data consists of circa four hours of interviews and two hours of observations (in the form of TaCs), where each interview took 56 minutes and each observation additional 34 minutes on average.

The interviews provided an overview of researchers' workflows, challenges and inefficiencies. This also included issues encountered with pre-existing software. The Think-Aloud Commentary on the other hand especially helped with detecting more specific difficulties, that are harder to remember during interview sessions. The interview script included questions such as the following:

- What are typical steps involved in research that deals with corpora/language variation?
- Can you tell us about the process of identifying and annotating linguistic elements?
- Do you currently use software for your work?

The interviews were recorded with both audio and video, transcribed, and finally augmented with manual notes taken during each interview session (step 2, Figure 1).

3.2 Data Analysis

We applied a Grounded Theory (GT) approach for qualitative data analysis (step 3, Figure 1).

In the first phase, we iteratively derived *codes*[1]. This iterative approach allowed us to compare *codes* with existing concepts and adjust the analysis as needed. This process repeatedly reinforced ideas and resolved conflicting concepts.

During the open coding stage, *codes* were independently extracted, then compared and reviewed in the axial coding stage. This method facilitated resolving uncertainties and conflicting *codes*, enhancing the results' quality.

[1] *Codes* are short key phrases that encapsulate singular concepts found in the data, see Section 2.3.

The analysis concluded with an *overarching theory*, formulated through the *core category* identified by the GT approach (step 4, Figure 1). This theory captures the most significant difficulties in corpus linguistics researchers' workflows and their underlying causes.

3.3 Identifying User Requirements

User requirements are derived to satisfy users' preferences, involving them continuously during the process (step 5, Figure 1). Therefore, it should be highlighted that user requirements are not to be misinterpreted as requirements held towards the user. They lay the foundation for conceptualizing and designing fitting solution ideas in later development stages.

4 Results

This section presents the findings from our Grounded Theory analysis, using open and axial coding to uncover key themes in language variation research (Section 4.1). We highlight the heavy reliance on manual processes and sparse use of software tools. A comprehensive summary is provided in Figure 2. The analysis identified central themes that guided us in understanding user requirements (see Section 4.2).

4.1 Data Analysis Results

After applying the *Open Coding* step on all of the collected data, we formulated 126 unique *codes* representing the main themes from interviews and observations. Each *code* was annotated with a participant identifier, capturing a wide variety of information for further analysis.

Grouping the *codes* for the second stage of the Grounded Theory approach (*Axial Coding*, Section 2.3) was done in two separate steps, which helped maintain a clear overview of the data. Firstly, the *codes* were classified into 12 broader groups[2], where each group contained 10-11 *codes* on average. This stage was concluded by identifying meaningful relations between the 12 general *code groups*, which enabled a comprehensive understanding of the overall concepts.

The formulated *codes* were collected in an Excel document (Microsoft Corporation, 2024) to further organize and prepare them for the next steps.

[2]A full overview of all general *code groups* that were derived from our analysis, as well the relations between them, is provided in the Appendix A.

4.1.1 Groups and Themes

The general *code groups* were formed by clustering together *codes* that share a collective theme and point to a common issue. The identified groups can be further abstracted and organized into broader themes, enabling a clearer structure and communication of our results. These themes include the common practice of *manually performing tasks*, the current *utilization of software assistance* tools, the *management of data*, and *further specific challenges* (i.e. creation, annotation, and analysis of the corpus) that occur *during* distinct steps of the *workflow*. Each of these themes covers a particular aspect of language variation research, for which the currently applied methodologies are sub-optimal or cause difficulties for researchers. The following paragraphs examine these broader themes to present the findings derived from the GT approach.

Performing Tasks Manually The implementation of manual, non-automated methodologies for performing tasks was not only prevalent throughout all interviews and observations, but it also significantly influenced and controlled every aspect throughout the progression of researchers' studies. Examples include tasks such as manually reading through the corpus and marking annotations, retrieving necessary information for the analysis by hand (i.e., by manually counting annotations), and only being able to update elements that occur multiple times in the corpus one instance at a time. Researchers also often encounter challenges with manual transcription, as exemplified by one interview-participant noting "For the transcription you sometimes need two hours to transcribe two minutes of spoken language. This makes you feel bad psychologically because you come home from work asking yourself what you have managed to do all day. Then you feel like a loser" (Interviewee #4). This reflection captures the exhaustive, slow process of manual transcription and emphasizes the psychological impact that frustrating manual work can impose. The execution of manual tasks therefore was found to be not only highly inefficient and error-prone but also placed a significant burden on the researchers who had to carry out these time-intensive activities.

Current Software Utilization Investigating current software utilization involves recognizing specific software applications that are currently used by researchers in the context of language varia-

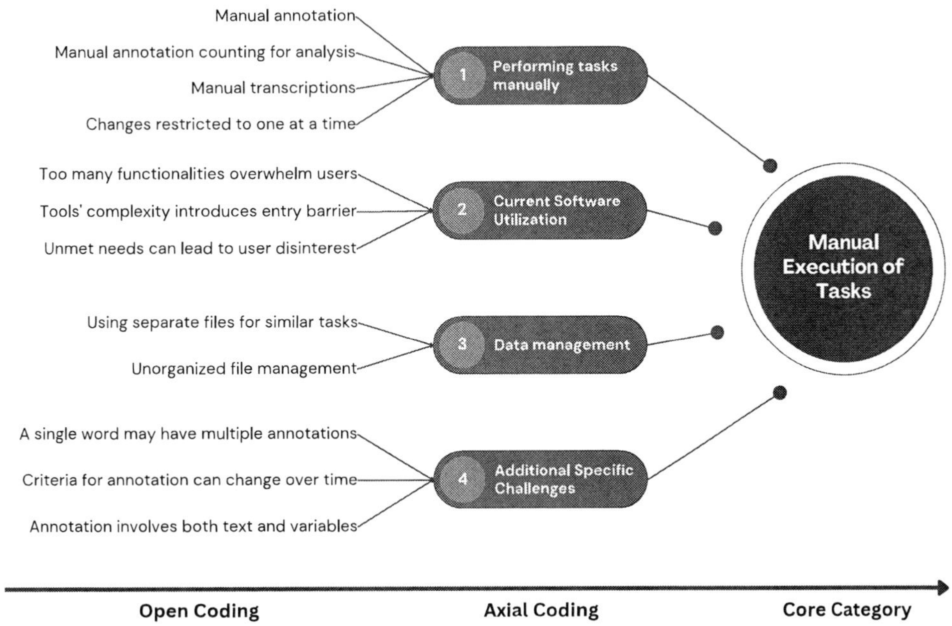

Figure 2: Stages of Analysis in the User-Centered Design Study: results from Open Coding to Axial Coding, ending with the identification of the Core Category. The process illustrates the refinement of data from initial findings to pinpointing the primary challenge of manual task execution in language research workflows.

tion studies, as well as identifying challenges they encounter while working with these tools. A representative selection of these tools was already introduced in Section 2.5. Software-related challenges primarily revolve around entry barriers that discourage the transition to digital tools. Our research indicates that these entry barriers are mainly shaped by the considerable time investment required to learn (and re-learn) the basic operations of software applications, as well as by a lack of intuitive methods for correctly importing existing data into the software. Additionally, researchers may also give up on using certain computer programs due to the software being incapable of fulfilling users' tasks and needs. One participant highlighted this issue by stating that "*Flex* felt like a software for non-linguists that need to do linguistic stuff, but it was not usable for my kind of research" (Interviewee #3). Lastly, our investigation revealed that researchers are frequently overwhelmed by tools offering an excessive amount of functionalities and interaction possibilities. This was clearly articulated by one of the participants who mentioned: "It's too much for me when programs have too many functions [...] would be good if a program is just reduced to the essentials" (Interviewee #4). This perspective highlights the discouragement they experience from either initiating or sustaining the use of a software application due to its complexity.

Data Management Our study also revealed widespread problems caused by researchers' data management. In this context, "data" includes information such as the corpus itself, speakers and their attributes, annotations in the corpus, and (intermediate) analysis results. We found that all of the interviewed researchers used different and independent files and locations for storing their data, sometimes even alternating between digital and analog environments. This practice frequently led to disorganized data structures, making navigation cumbersome and resulting in inconsistencies and critical errors in the stored data. Additionally, weak data management resulted in decreased research productivity and further demotivated researchers.

Further Challenges During Workflow The discussed themes highlighted universal challenges impacting all aspects of language variation studies, alongside unique issues specific to certain tasks. A key finding is the significant interconnection between these general and specific challenges; for example, data management problems can worsen annotation difficulties by limiting access to crucial context. Addressing these interconnected challenges is essential for developing effective design solutions and ensuring the usability of the application.

4.1.2 Core Category

Considering all of the extracted data, challenges, and themes, our research identified the manual execution of tasks as the *core category* and primary source for existing difficulties in language variation studies. As previously mentioned, manual task execution was implemented by all researchers during a majority of their workflows and tasks in our interviews, thus negatively influencing every aspect of their research process. Given this extensive influence, we assessed that no other practice or methodology had a greater impact on its efficiency.

Identifying this core category implies the necessity of automated software solutions addressing these manual task challenges.

4.2 User Requirements

The insights obtained from the previous steps can be used to specify relevant user requirements. These requirements are derived from the specific problems and needs of the target user group and should therefore be fulfilled by the intended design solution. This section lists a selection of the most essential requirements evoked from our user study.

4.2.1 Relevant Requirements for Design Solutions

Our user research enabled the formulation of a total of 14 primary user requirements[3], with our attention directed towards reporting on the four most significant ones.

(i) *Ensuring intuitive usability* is a fundamental criterion for the design solution. The tool's user interface must provide intuitive interactions, tailored to the target users' knowledge and skills, emphasizing simplicity and focusing on essential features. This approach addresses challenges highlighted in prior user studies, guiding the requirements derivation process. (ii) Better *data-management-systems* stems from the identified data management issues. A data(base)-management system simplifies the interaction between the user and the database by ensuring consistency and managing all data-flows automatically (Dumas et al., 2018). A solution that incorporates such a system can effectively resolve data-related issues, freeing users from the responsibility of managing data storage and ensuring its consistency. (iii) *Digital Annotation* enhances the research process by automating (part of) the annotation tasks within a digital environment. This feature ensures uniform annotations across the corpus, thereby facilitating a more robust analysis. It also allows for the annotation of multiple elements simultaneously, significantly increasing productivity. Moreover, digital annotation can provide immediate feedback to users on the impact of their actions on the corpus, leading to more consistent and correct user actions. (iv) *Automatic Analysis* leverages digital annotations to enable fast, error-free counting and evaluation of data. Automatic analysis significantly facilitates research by efficiently collecting and assessing corpus annotations. This automation supports the execution of complex quantitative and statistical analyses.

[3]See Appendix C.1 for a list of the 14 primary user requirements, and Appendix C.2 for additional research directions.

4.2.2 Limitations

The limitations in meeting user requirements stem not only from technical constraints but also from the diverse personal preferences of users, leading to highly individualized approaches that make it hard to establish a set of requirements catering to all user needs. This was particularly evident in manual annotation tasks within our user study, where each participant employed a unique method for tagging linguistic features, none of which were efficient due to their manual nature. This diversity complicates the creation of uniform user requirements. While standardizing processes could offer a solution by setting expected standards, it restricts user freedom and may not fully satisfy everyone, though it could help address the broader issue more uniformly.

5 Future Directions: Engaging Users in Design and Development

Even after gathering user requirements, continuing to incorporate user feedback is crucial throughout the design and implementation phases of software development. The initial concept stage focuses on developing design solutions based on previously identified user needs, as well as employing prototypes to test and refine created design solutions. This approach ensures that the design effectively meets user expectations and informs the implementation process in later stages of development.

5.1 Concepts and Sketches

One way of starting the development of potential software solutions is by creating *sketches* (step 6, Figure 1). Sketches are essential tools for visualizing and refining ideas, serving as a bridge between initial concepts and final designs (Tversky et al., 2003). They are encouraged to be hand-drawn, quickly made, and easily disposable, which means that each sketch has a very low cost (for an example of a sketch, see Appendix D.1). Therefore, sketching allows for rapid exploration of solution concepts, as well as evaluating and communicating these results (Greenberg et al., 2011), which makes it a powerful technique for our purpose. Easy communication through sketches allows for sharing comprehensible design ideas (i.e., with the target user group). This enables collaborative refinement of the sketches based on user feedback, which if performed iteratively (Simon, 1969) leads to converging to a specific design solution in the form of a low-fidelity-prototype (step 7, Figure 1).

5.2 Prototypes

Low-fidelity prototypes (see Appendix D.2) serve as an initial representation of the design solution concept and have been found to be extremely useful throughout the product development cycle (Virzi et al., 1996). Unlike their high-fidelity counterparts, these prototypes are not expected to replicate the final product's look or functionality fully. Instead, they can be rapidly created without losing their utility (Walker et al., 2002), facilitating the exploration of various conceptual designs and enhancing the ease of sharing these ideas for user research (Sharp et al., 2019).

Similar to the refinement of sketches, prototypes can also be refined as part of an iterative process. This process includes cycles of user feedback and fidelity enhancement that aim at ultimately creating a high-fidelity (software) prototype. High-fidelity prototypes should look and behave like the finished product, which means that they should also be close to fully functional (step 8, Figure 1). Maintaining user involvement during fidelity enhancement ensures that the resulting software remains tailored to user preferences and requirements (Sharp et al., 2019) (step 9, Figure 1).

5.3 Implementation

As a final step, our aim is to transition from a high-fidelity prototype to usable software (step 10, Figure 1). To increase the speed of development, the final software will be built on top of the functionalities presented in *CorpusCompass* (Adnan and Brandizzi, 2023). This digital tool, initially developed for corpus linguistics research, primarily focuses on automatic analysis of text-based corpora, a key component for language variation studies. Our data analysis indicates that *CorpusCompass* fulfills several user requirements identified for our project, making it a valuable technical foundation. Despite its importance, *CorpusCompass* was not developed with a focus on user needs, resulting in a user interface that is lacking in functionality and usability. To make it more useful, it is essential to conduct additional user studies and develop an interface that facilitates easy interaction. Thus better serving the needs of sociolinguists by linking advanced linguistic analysis with practical usability.

6 Conclusion

Sociolinguists studying language variation in under-resourced languages often lack supporting software tools. Addressing this requires an interdisciplinary perspective across Sociolinguistics and Human-Computer Interaction. This paper provides such a perspective and actualizes it with a UCD approach.

Our empirical work is motivated to understand, respect, and support the unique requirements of sociolinguists in their workflows. To this end, we collected rich qualitative data through interviews and observations with various academics researching language variation. Our participants were recruited from different academic institutions in Europe, and all focus on studying Arabic dialects.

This data revealed key challenges that sociolinguists encounter during their work, arising from the practice of error-prone manual text analysis and inconsistent data management approaches. The underlying root cause is a lack of software tools tailored to meet sociolinguists' specific requirements in the context of language variation research. This leads to further difficulties and inefficiencies during the research process. It is important to note that sociolinguists studying different languages, particularly those without formal writing systems, or working in different academic contexts, may face unique challenges that require tailored solutions. Thus, while our study provides valuable insights, it may not encompass all the needs of sociolinguistic researchers worldwide.

Based on these insights, we specified a set of concrete user requirements, which serve as a guideline for the design and development of better software tools. By introducing the idea of sketches and prototypes, we have illustrated how these requirements can be leveraged constructively. We plan to implement these ideas in a functional open-source tool. Beyond our specific study here, we hope that this paper stimulates interdisciplinary perspectives to facilitate the often overlooked practical side of sociolinguistic research work.

References

Chadia Abras, Diane Maloney-Krichmar, Jenny Preece, et al. 2004. User-centered design. *Bainbridge, W. Encyclopedia of Human-Computer Interaction. Thousand Oaks: Sage Publications*, 37(4):445–456.

Oliver Adams, Trevor Cohn, Graham Neubig, Hilaria Cruz, Steven Bird, and Alexis Michaud. 2019. Evaluating phonemic transcription of low-resource tonal languages for language documentation. In *11th International Conference on Language Resources and Evaluation, LREC 2018*, pages 3356–3365. European Language Resources Association (ELRA).

Muhadj Adnan and Nicolo' Brandizzi. 2023. Corpuscompass: A tool for data extraction and dataset generation in corpus linguistics. In *Proceedings of the 9th Italian Conference on Computational Linguistics*, volume 3596, pages 16–27, Venice, Italy. CEUR Workshop Proceedings.

Roobaea Alroobaea and Pam J Mayhew. 2014. How many participants are really enough for usability studies? In *2014 Science and Information Conference*, pages 48–56. IEEE.

Robert Bayley. 2013. *The Quantitative Paradigm*, chapter 4. John Wiley & Sons, Ltd.

D. Biber, S. Conrad, and R. Reppen. 1998. *Corpus Linguistics: Investigating Language Structure and Use*. Cambridge Approaches to Linguistics. Cambridge University Press.

Steven Bird. 2021. Sparse Transcription. *Computational Linguistics*, 46(4):713–744.

Bharathi Raja Chakravarthi, Mihael Arcan, and John P. McCrae. 2019. Comparison of Different Orthographies for Machine Translation of Under-Resourced Dravidian Languages. In *2nd Conference on Language, Data and Knowledge (LDK 2019)*, volume 70 of *Open Access Series in Informatics (OASIcs)*, pages 6:1–6:14, Dagstuhl, Germany. Schloss Dagstuhl – Leibniz-Zentrum für Informatik.

Juliet M. Corbin and Anselm Strauss. 1990. Grounded theory research: Procedures, canons, and evaluative criteria. *Qualitative sociology*, 13(1):3–21.

Deborah Cotton and Karen Gresty. 2006. Reflecting on the think-aloud method for evaluating e-learning. *British Journal of Educational Technology*, 37(1):45–54.

Organización Internacional de Normalización. 2010. *Ergonomics of Human-system Interaction: Human-centred Design for Interactive Systems*. ISO.

Marlon Dumas, Marcello La Rosa, Jan Mendling, Hajo A Reijers, et al. 2018. *Fundamentals of business process management*, volume 2. Springer.

Saul Greenberg, Sheelagh Carpendale, Nicolai Marquardt, and Bill Buxton. 2011. *Sketching user experiences: The workbook*. Elsevier.

Gregory Guy. 2013. *Words and numbers: quantitative analysis in sociolinguistics*, pages 194–210. Wiley-Blackwell.

Dongseop Kwon, Sun Kim, Chih-Hsuan Wei, Robert Leaman, and Zhiyong Lu. 2018. eztag: tagging biomedical concepts via interactive learning. *Nucleic Acids Research*, 46(W1):W523–W529.

William Labov. 2006. *The Social Stratification of English in New York City*, 2 edition. Cambridge University Press.

Travis Lowdermilk. 2013. *User-centered design: a developer's guide to building user-friendly applications*. " O'Reilly Media, Inc.".

Christian Mair. 2018. *1 .Erfolgsgeschichte Korpuslinguistik?*, pages 5–26. De Gruyter, Berlin, Boston.

Microsoft Corporation. 2024. Microsoft Excel. Computer Software.

Mariana Neves and Jurica Ševa. 2019. An extensive review of tools for manual annotation of documents. *Briefings in Bioinformatics*, 22(1):146–163.

J. Nielsen. 2012. Thinking aloud: The# 1 usability tool. Last accessed 21 February 2024.

Surangika Ranathunga, En-Shiun Annie Lee, Marjana Prifti Skenduli, Ravi Shekhar, Mehreen Alam, and Rishemjit Kaur. 2023. Neural machine translation for low-resource languages: A survey. *ACM Computing Surveys*, 55(11):1–37.

E Frank Ritter, D Gordon Baxter, and F Elizabeth Churchill. 2014. *Foundations for designing user-centered systems: What system designers need to know about people*. Springer.

H. Sharp, J. Preece, and Y. Rogers. 2019. *Interaction Design: Beyond Human-Computer Interaction*. Wiley.

Herbert A. Simon. 1969. *The Sciences of the Artificial*. The MIT Press.

Pontus Stenetorp, Sampo Pyysalo, Goran Topić, Tomoko Ohta, Sophia Ananiadou, and Jun'ichi Tsujii. 2012. brat: a web-based tool for NLP-assisted text annotation. In *Proceedings of the Demonstrations at the 13th Conference of the European Chapter of the Association for Computational Linguistics*, pages 102–107, Avignon, France. Association for Computational Linguistics.

Sali A Tagliamonte. 2006. *Analysing sociolinguistic variation*. Cambridge University Press.

Barbara Tversky, Masaki Suwa, Maneesh Agrawala, Julie Heiser, Chris Stolte, Pat Hanrahan, Doantam Phan, Jeff Klingner, Marie-Paule Daniel, Paul Lee, et al. 2003. Sketches for design and design of sketches. *Human Behaviour in Design: Individuals, Teams, Tools*, pages 79–86.

Robert A Virzi, Jeffrey L Sokolov, and Demetrios Karis. 1996. Usability problem identification using both low-and high-fidelity prototypes. In *Proceedings of the SIGCHI conference on human factors in computing systems*, pages 236–243.

James A. Walker. 2012. *Variation in Linguistic Systems*. Routledge.

Miriam Walker, Leila Takayama, and James A Landay. 2002. High-fidelity or low-fidelity, paper or computer? choosing attributes when testing web prototypes. In *Proceedings of the human factors and ergonomics society annual meeting*, volume 46, pages 661–665. Sage Publications Sage CA: Los Angeles, CA.

Guillaume Wisniewski, Alexis Michaud, and Séverine Guillaume. 2020. Phonemic transcription of low-resource languages: To what extent can preprocessing be automated? In *1st Joint SLTU (Spoken Language Technologies for Under-resourced languages) and CCURL (Collaboration and Computing for Under-Resourced Languages) Workshop*, pages 306–315. European Language Resources Association (ELRA).

Seid Muhie Yimam, Iryna Gurevych, Richard Eckart de Castilho, and Chris Biemann. 2013. WebAnno: A flexible, web-based and visually supported system for distributed annotations. In *Proceedings of the 51st Annual Meeting of the Association for Computational Linguistics: System Demonstrations*, pages 1–6, Sofia, Bulgaria. Association for Computational Linguistics.

Claudia Zapata and José Antonio Pow-Sang. 2012. Sample size in a heuristic evaluation of usability. *Software Engineering: Methods, Modeling, and Teaching*, 37.

Appendix

A Axial Coding Results and Thematic Relationships

Figure 3 presents a visualization of the twelve *code groups* extracted from the axial coding stage, as part of Grounded Theory methodology. This illustration is designed to enhance clarity by focusing on the most critical relationships and *code groups* from the data. In the provided context, the *variables* (colored in turquoise) signify specific linguistic features (*Dependent Variables*) or speaker attributes (*Independent Variables*).[4]

As can be seen from the figure, data management is a key challenge in research workflows, directly impacting the creation of variables and the efficiency of annotation. It contrasts manual, error-prone tasks with the potential for increased efficiency and reduced errors through automated processes, underscoring our findings that automation is a desirable, though not yet fully realized, goal in language variation research. The diagram further delineates the ripple effect of data management on research output. Effective management is shown to allow for the incorporation of more variables, which can lead to richer, more nuanced research. However, this also introduces a trade-off between the potential benefits of having more variables and the additional effort required to manage them.

B Research Interests of the Users

For our study, we interviewed four participants with different academic positions, different universities, and fields of research (Table 1). The research conducted by our participants encompasses a wide range of topics within the field of Arabic sociolinguistics, primarily focusing on how language behavior varies across different social contexts, speaker backgrounds, and geographic regions. This includes for instance the study of how individuals adapt their language in response to their surroundings and interaction partners (known as language accommodation) and the differences in speech patterns between native and second language (L2) speakers. Moreover, the research focuses on the linguistic diversity found in densely populated areas, particularly examining the variation between formal and informal Arabic, the impact of identity on language use, and the influence of regional dialects on over-regional language. For example, one of the participants explores the complex environment of Morocco's multilingual setting, focusing on the diverse facets of language that such a context presents. The participants worked mainly on phonological, morphological, and lexical features occurring in their data. From a sociolinguistic perspective, these studies shed light on the complex relationship between language, society, and identity, highlighting the diverse ways in which language functions both as a tool for communication and as a marker of cultural and individual identity. The complexity of annotating, processing, and analyzing such data underscores the need for flexible tools that can accommodate the uniqueness of each research area, as every researcher's requirements differ considerably.

ID	Academic Position	Affiliation
#1	Assistant Professor	University of Bayreuth, Germany
#2	Postdoctoral Researcher	University of Bergamo, Italy
#3	Postdoctoral Researcher	Freie Universität Berlin, Germany
#4	Ph.D. Candidate	University of Vienna, Austria

Table 1: Overview of User Study Participants by Academic Position and Affiliation.

C Further User Requirements

This section documents all identified user requirements, as well as further requirements that we will not pursue but that inspire further research.

C.1 Full List of Implementable User Requirements

The following list captures the 14 user requirements that were derived from analysing the data from the user interviews and observations. Each requirement is followed by a short description detailing the expectations for a User-Centered Design solution.

1. Data/Variable-Management-System: Enables consistent data/variable-changes
2. Digital Annotation: Digitally enhanced manual annotation
3. Ensure intuitive software usability: Interactions must be relevant and intuitive
4. Automated analysis: Automatic variable and annotation counting

[4]While extralinguistic variables are used here exclusively as predictors, it is important to note that not all linguistic variables are dependent. The basic principle of the study of variation is that linguistic context often contributes significantly to variational preferences.

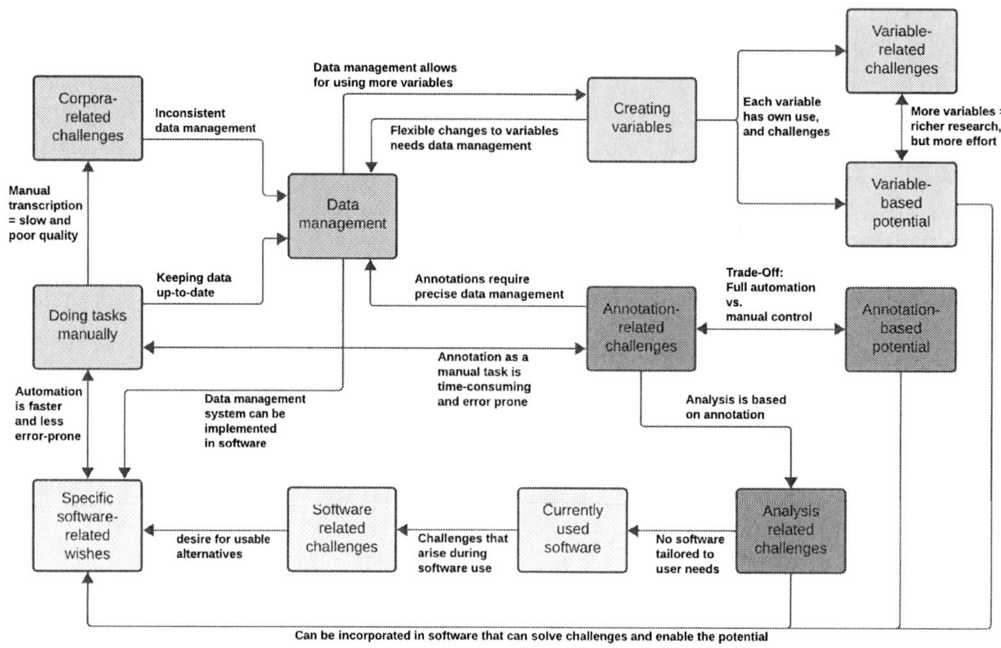

Figure 3: Illustration of *code* relationships from axial coding in Grounded Theory, focusing on data management as the core challenge in research workflows. The diagram shows its impact on variable creation, annotation efficiency, and the need for software that aligns with user needs. It highlights trade-offs between manual and automated annotation, as well as the potential for richer research through variable diversity.

5. Customizing annotation format: System detects individual annotations
6. Detect multiple annotations: Detect words with multiple annotations
7. (Partially) automatic annotation: Controlled automation of annotation process
8. Search/Highlight annotations: Enable finding annotations quickly
9. Data-Viewer: Intuitive representation of analysis results
10. Automated text-to-speaker-mapping: Detect speaker-text-correspondence
11. Corpus Management: Load and remove text files from corpus
12. Clear and intuitive navigation: Overlay that allows clear navigation
13. Corpus Exploration Section: Check whole corpus for correctness
14. Automatic variable extraction: Automatically extract data from corpus

Based on the list, Requirements 1 to 8 directly represent user needs identified during data analysis. In contrast, Requirements 9 to 14 serve as follow-up requirements, indirectly fulfilling user needs by facilitating the implementation of Requirements 1 to 8 in a technical context (for example, *10. Automated text-to-speaker mapping* enables *4. Automated analysis* by associating spoken text with speakers, thus facilitating the identification of patterns in language use).

C.2 Additional Research Directions in User Requirements

We identified additional requirements that, due to their high complexity and effort-to-benefit ratio, will not be pursued in the current project scope. Furthermore, additional user studies would be necessary to develop a sufficient design solution that fully addresses all facets of these intricate requirements. However, we documented two of them here to inform future research and highlight areas for deeper exploration.

(i) *Automatic Transcription* involves converting spoken language from audio recordings into written text. This process is traditionally labor-intensive, posing a significant time investment due to the lack of effective automation options, particularly for under-resourced languages. Despite recent advancements and growing interest in this field (Adams et al., 2019), substantial challenges (differences in phonemic inventories, phonotactic combinations, and word structure between languages, as well as limited training data for accurate transcription models) persist, as highlighted by recent research (Wisniewski et al., 2020). An intuitive and efficient design solution for automatic transcription could significantly enhance the efficiency of language variation studies by reducing manual effort and time. (ii) *Automatic and Reliable Corpus Translation* faces similar complexities, primarily relying on manual translation efforts. The challenge lies in achieving consistent and accurate translations across diverse language corpora, a task that continues to be difficult, given the complexity of linguistic variations (Ranathunga et al., 2023). Developing a design solution that ensures intuitive use, consistent processing, and reliable outcomes for corpus translation could dramatically expand the research capabilities in language variation studies, making it more accessible and less time-consuming.

D Sketches and Prototypes

While sketches and low-fidelity prototypes may appear similar initially, a difference in their purpose can be outlined. For our design process, sketching is intended for the exploration of a variety of design ideas, whereas prototyping focuses on the refinement of promising design concepts.

D.1 Sketches

Figure 4 shows an example of a sketch. It illustrates how sketches are characterized by a low level of detail and quick creation, as well as being easily disposable due to the little effort for creating them. This enables the exploration of many different design solution ideas that can be vastly different, while also allowing communication and evaluation of basic components and concepts.

D.2 Prototypes

Figure 5 portrays a (low-fidelity) prototype that is informed by the identified user requirements. It expands on earlier sketches by refining ideas and increasing the level of detail, enabling a clearer communication and evaluation, especially with target users. To incorporate functionality, a "slide-based" prototype can be employed, where each slide represents a state of the design solution (for instance, a software) by using detailed, drawn images, which

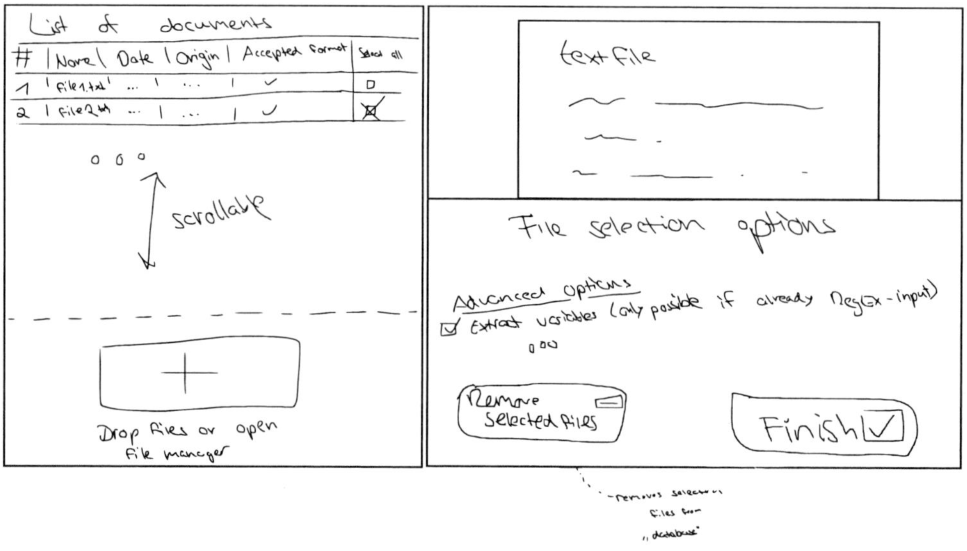

Figure 4: Illustration of a potential design solution sketch for managing corpus files, highlighting how sketching encourages the exploration of design solutions in the context of User-Centered Design.

are interconnected through linked elements in the slides.

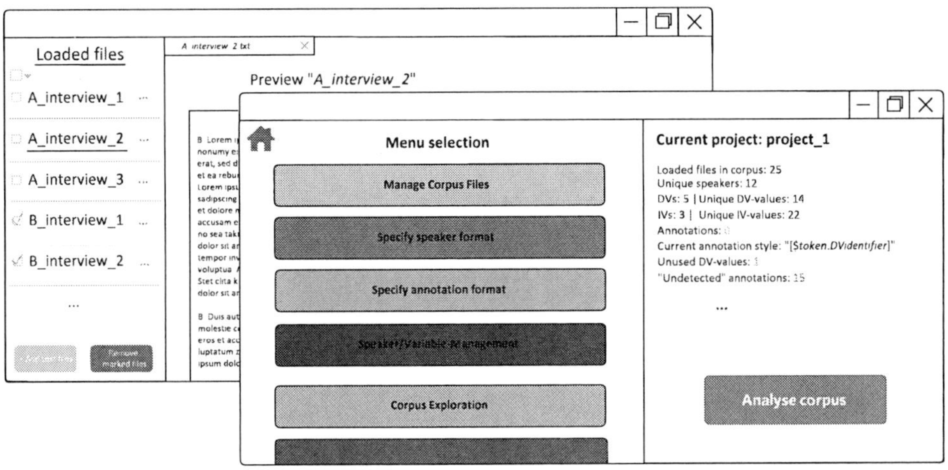

Figure 5: Refined drawing portraying a (low-fidelity) prototype, which can be used to communicate design solutions and obtain feedback during additional user studies.

Documenting Endangered Languages with *LangDoc*: A Wordlist-Based System and A Case Study on Moklen

Piyapath T Spencer
Faculty of Arts, Chulalongkorn University
linguistics@piyapath.uk

Abstract

Language documentation, especially languages lacking standardised writing systems, is a laborious and time-consuming process. This paper introduces *LangDoc*, a comprehensive system designed to address challenges and improve the efficiency and accuracy of language documentation projects. LangDoc offers several features, including tools for managing, recording, and reviewing the collected data. It operates both online and offline, crucial for fieldwork in remote locations. The paper also presents a comparative analysis demonstrating LangDoc's efficiency compared to other methods. A case study of the Moklen language documentation project demonstrates how the features address the specific challenges of working with endangered languages and remote communities. Future development areas include integrating with NLP tools for advanced linguistic analysis and emphasising its potential to support the preservation of language diversity.

1 Introduction

Amongst the very first tasks in language documentation are to collect and record vocabulary of the language. Traditionally, language data have been collected and stored in its most primitive form, often involving manual recording on paper or default word lists, sometimes with audio recording. This process is yet the most gruelling and labour-intensive. Despite the use of technology and/or computer-assisted systems in latter studies (e.g. Black and Simons (2006), Yooyen (2013), Dunham (2014), van Esch et al. (2019)), the heavy reliance on humans is inevitable, especially converting field notes into computer-stored data prior to any further analyses.

Human errors normally weaken the efficiency of a documentation project and contributes to various issues within the system (cf. Rasmussen and Vicente (1989), Compton (2014)), including compromising the overall quality of the information obtained, regardless of the limited resources and other constraints. *LangDoc*[1] is then a system designed to streamline the recording and analysing process of the language data whilst mitigating errors associated with human involvement in collaborative projects, specifically for such languages including but not limited to which lacking conventionalised writing systems. Its functionality extends to both online and offline environments, making it particularly well-suited for language documentation conducted in remote locations.

In particular, this paper presents its idea, as well as system design, functionalities and features. It will also discuss the system's current limitations and outline the possible direction for future development. To illustrate the functionalities, this paper demonstrates LangDoc with a real-world use case by its application in documenting the Moklen in the Southern Thailand.

This paper makes several key contributions to the field of language documentation. Firstly, it aims to address common challenges faced in this domain, such as managing data from multiple sources, logistical difficulties in collaborative teamwork, and also extending to tackle such external limitations as the well-being of language informants. Secondly, the paper proposes features to mitigate common errors and enhance the efficacy, whilst acknowledging the essential role of trained linguists. Thirdly, the paper presents offline synchronisation feature is crucial for fieldwork in remote locations. The system allows users to collect data without an internet connection and syncs automatically when connectivity is restored. Additionally, the system's architecture allows for future integration with tools for deeper linguistic analysis to further expand its capabilities.

[1]The online system can be found at `https://langdoc.piyapath.uk`. For the offline programme and any other inquiries, feel free to contact the author.

Proceedings of the 3rd Workshop on NLP Applications to Field Linguistics (Field Matters 2024), pages 28–36
August 16, 2024 ©2024 Association for Computational Linguistics

2 Background Issues and Related Work

Collecting vocabulary data for endangered languages presents significant challenges, particularly when the documentation effort is led by community outsiders. The conventional approach of conducting interviews and elicitation sessions with native speaker informants can be inefficient, costly, and potentially detrimental to the well-being of elderly informants who often serve as the primary sources of linguistic knowledge.

One of the major issues is the limited productivity of data collection sessions, especially with elderly informants who may have physical limitations. As observed in Moklen fieldwork, interviews with elders typically yield a maximum of 60 words per session, with several breaks required within a three-hour period. Completing a modest vocabulary list of 250 words can take at least five days of work, and more extensive projects naturally require even greater resource investment.

Another challenge arises when multiple researchers are involved in the documentation effort. Dividing informant interviews amongst project members can lead to wasted effort due to duplicate recordings of common vocabulary and the potential to miss more specific, culturally-related terms known to certain informants; not to mention the additional time to be spent merging data and identifying missing entries.

Furthermore, inconsistencies in the interpretations by different researchers can arise, especially when dealing with a semantically complex spoken languages like Moklen. To resolve these discrepancies often requires revisiting informants in person, hindering the overall progress. Even if larger team appear to be bring a faster data collection, the unique challenges of endangered language documentation suggest that a more focused approach tailored to the needs of the specific community is crucial. Overwhelming elderly informants with lots of people can lead to shorter, less productive sessions due to factors such as fatigue and discomfort.

In recent years, there have been efforts to integrate technologies for recording, transcribing, and analysing language records (Rice and Thieberger, 2018), as well as other NLP tasks (Moeller et al., 2024; Serikov et al., 2023) to language documentation. Nevertheless, most works focus on how can the data can be used to represent linguistic phenomena; little attention, however, has been given to tackle the fundamental problem of how linguists or researchers can actually and effectively collect and prepare the necessary linguistic data in the first place, especially for endangered languages with rapidly dwindling speaker populations. Of course, good tools and applications have emerged to aid in field linguistics, such as Aikuma (Bird et al., 2014), FLEx (Zook, 2024), and ELAN (Max Planck Institute for Psycholinguistics, 2023), yet often operate in silos and do not comprehensively address the multifaceted challenges faced by linguists in the field. There is a need for solutions that holistically address the data collection process whilst considering the unique logistical, ethical and community-related challenges faced when documenting such endangered languages.

The issues highlighted above point to a primary use case that the proposed system aims to address, comprising a team of field linguists with varying experience working to document the vocabulary of an endangered language spoken by a remote community with few population of elderly native speakers. In the scenario when the opportunities to work with remaining fluent speakers are increasingly limited, efficiently and sensitively collecting high-quality data are paramount.

3 The LangDoc System

LangDoc is a comprehensive system designed to streamline the language documentation process, particularly for endangered languages lacking standardised writing systems. It incorporates several key features to address the challenges identified in the background section.

3.1 Wordlist-driven Recording System

Although wordlist-driven recording is a standard practice in language documentation, LangDoc introduces significant improvements where users have their flexibility to create and customise the wordlist-based project and propose the structured workflow that minimise the complexity of working process. Unlike existing tools, LangDoc's design ensures that all entries are systematically reviewed and verified, which is particularly important in the context of endangered languages with limited speaker populations.

3.1.1 Wordlist Management

LangDoc provides a comprehensive wordlist management interface that allows users to create, edit, and organise wordlists within their projects (cf. subsubsection 3.2.1).

3.1.2 Entry Management

Each wordlist consists of individual word entries, stored in the `entry` table of the database. This table maintains information about each entry, such field as the word form, its part of speech (POS), definition, category, and its working status.

Users can add new entries to a wordlist by filling out a form that captures fields such as headword, POS, category, and meaning. Not every field is required, as users can customise the fields according to their needs. The reason for this is to accommodate various use cases of specific projects, such as creating a dictionary for the community.

3.1.3 Data Collection

The wordlist-driven recording system provides a structured and organised approach to word collection by presenting users with a list of wordlists and their associated entries. Users with the `collector` role can access the *To Collect* section, which displays wordlists that have unrecorded entries.

For each wordlist, collectors can view the percentage of entries that have been recorded, providing an overview of the progress made. By clicking on a wordlist, users are redirected to a dedicated page where they can record pronunciation data (IPA) for each entry.

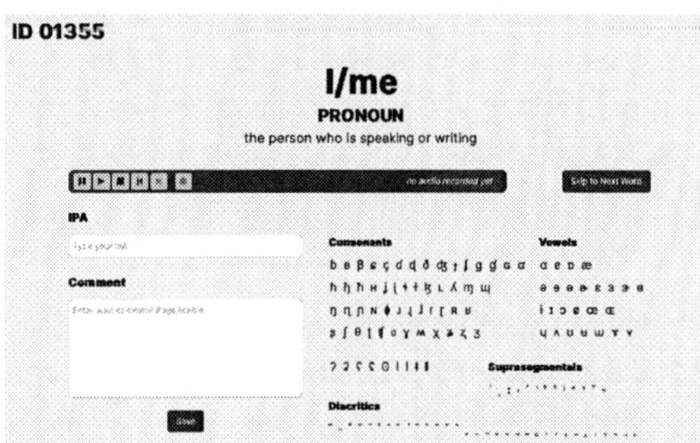

Figure 1: Sample recording interface

The data collection interface, as in Figure 1, presents the word entries sequentially, allowing users to input the IPA transcription using a character picker, add comments or notes, and navigate between entries within a wordlist. The system, however, prioritises audio recordings of words. Specifically, collectors can only record audio for each entry without providing IPA or notes. This approach helps mitigate potential biases compared to hasty transcriptions by collectors. Users also have the option to skip entries or mark them for review.

3.1.4 Instant Word Collection

In addition to the wordlist-driven approach, LangDoc offers an "Instant Word Collection" feature that enables users to quickly gather words from informants without associating them with specific wordlists in the project.

The interface is similar to normal word collection in that it allows users to record information about particular words. However, this feature also gives users more flexibility, including to either select existing informants or add new ones, to enter the head word or morpheme, and then to record the word, along with optional IPA transcription and comments.

3.2 Project Management Tools

LangDoc also provides robust project management tools, allowing users to create new projects, assign project members with specific roles (i.e. `admin`, `collector`, `analyser`), and manage project settings and preferences.

3.2.1 Project Creation

The project creation process in LangDoc is designed to be straightforward. Users can initiate the creation of a new project by providing essential information such as the project name, affiliation, and the language under study. An autocomplete feature assists users in selecting the language by suggesting matching language names or ISO 639-3 codes (International Organization for Standardization, 2007) as they type.

Once the basic project information is provided, users can choose to associate one of the existing wordlists, as shown in Table 1, with the project. Prior to the modification to include semantic category and meaning for dictionary representation, those predefined wordlists below only offer headwords and their part of speech. The other way is to proceed without a wordlist, as the customised lists can be later imported as CSV or XLSX to the project. This flexibility allows users to tailor the project setup according to their specific requirements.

After selecting the suitable wordlist, the project creator can also add people whose the LangDoc account exists within the current database to the creating project. By and large, all project settings and preferences aside from the basic information are optional and can be altered afterward.

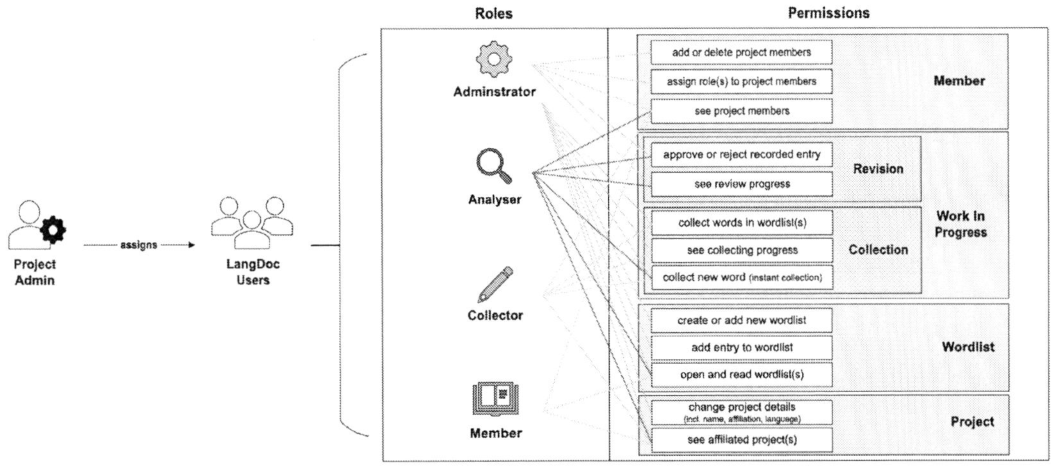

Figure 2: An RBAC diagram showing roles within a project in the LangDoc system

Wordlist	Citation
Swadesh 100	Swadesh (1971)
Swadesh 207	Swadesh (1952)
ASJP 40	Wichmann et al. (2007)
Swadesh-Yakhontov 35	Starostin (1991)
Dolgopolsky 15	Dolgopolsky (1964, 1986)
CALMSEA	Matisoff (1978)
NGSL 1.2	Browne et al. (2023)
Sign Language	Emmorey and Lane (2000)

Table 1: Predefined wordlists available in LangDoc

3.2.2 Project Assignment

LangDoc applies a role-based access control system (RBAC) to manage project members and their permissions. The project creator is automatically assigned the administrator role, which allows assigning roles with specific access levels to other members. Each user can have multiple roles within a project and roles can vary across different projects.

As illustrated in Figure 2, the available roles within a project include:

- **Project Admin**: Administrators have full control over the project, including managing members, data analysis, and data storage.
- **Analyser**: Members assigned the `analyser` role are responsible for reviewing and analysing the collected linguistic data to determine its usability and accuracy.
- **Collector**: The `collector` role involves recording and managing the collected linguistic data within the project.
- **Member**: General members have limited access and are participants in the project with standard privileges.

By assigning specific roles, LangDoc secures that the right individuals have the necessary permissions to perform their designated tasks, maintaining data security and efficient project management.

3.2.3 Project Management

LangDoc provides a dedicated project management interface that allows administrators to oversee and manage various aspects of their projects. This interface includes:

- **Project Settings**: Administrators can access and modify project preferences, including general project details and other customisation options.
- **Wordlist Management**: Administrators can create new wordlists and add entries to existing wordlists for the whole project.
- **Member Management**: Administrators can add or remove project members, as well as modify their assigned roles within the project.
- **Progress Tracking**: The project management interface provides an overview of the progress made on each wordlist, displaying the percentage of entries that have been recorded or require revision.

Through these comprehensive project management tools, LangDoc allows administrators to effectively coordinate and oversee linguistic data collection and analysis projects for the organised working environment. Whilst this section is dedicated for project administrators, some discussed functionalities can overlap across roles as seen in Figure 2.

3.3 Collaborative Review System

To enhance the quality and accuracy of the data, LangDoc includes a collaborative review system that allows senior members designated as `analysers` to collectively review, verify and refine the recorded data. Their primary tasks include listening to recorded pronunciations, verifying transcription accuracy, and making necessary corrections or annotations, so as to maintain the integrity and accuracy of the linguistic data that meet the research objectives.

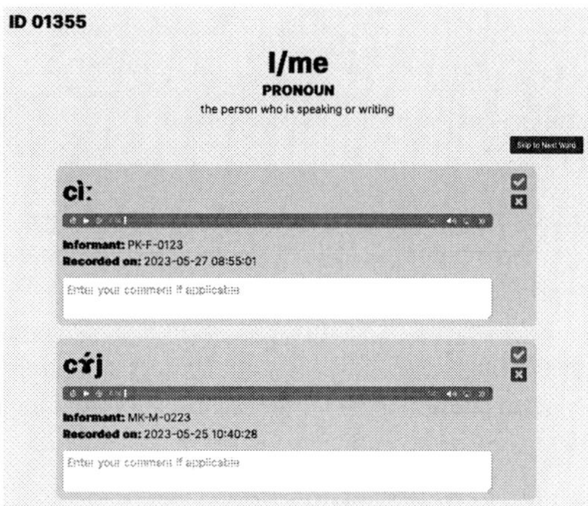

Figure 3: Sample review interface (1SG in Moklen)

The review interface in LangDoc is intuitively designed to facilitate an efficient review process. It presents all the data entries that require verification in a listed format, allowing analysers to easily navigate through them. Each entry includes detailed information such as the word, its phonetic transcription, and any notes or comments added by the collector.

Analysers can play audio recordings directly within the interface and compare them against the provided transcriptions. If discrepancies or errors are found, analysers can edit the transcriptions directly in the interface. They also have the option to add detailed comments to provide context or justification for the changes they make.

3.3.1 Collaborative Features

To promote collaboration, LangDoc includes several features that support real-time communication and data sharing amongst analysers, aside from the automatic status tagging system:

- **Commenting System**: Analysers can leave comments visible to all members on each entry to discuss discrepancies, suggest alternatives, or provide insights.
- **Change Tracking**: The system keeps a log of all changes made to each entry, including who made the change and when, to maintain transparency and accountability in the process.
- **Consensus Building**: For entries that require further discussion, analysers can flag them for review to ultimately build consensus on the most accurate transcription as the final decision.

3.4 Data Transfer

Another critical feature of the LangDoc system is its comprehensive data transfer functionality. This feature is provided due to the fact that LangDoc is designed as a tool, rather than a closed platform, to address the diverse needs of linguistic researchers and project teams for their recorded language data. It allows them to use their available data in the system, and to access and utilise their data outside the LangDoc environment.

Apart from its import functionality discussed in subsubsection 3.2.1 to serve users who are more familiar with data in other formats, The LangDoc system allows users to have complete access to their project's information via the export of various types of data, including recorded wordlists, audio recordings, and relevant metadata. Users initiate the export process by selecting the specific project or wordlist they wish to export. This ranges from the selection of specific wordlists to the entire project data. It also supports multiple export formats (i.e. CSV, JSON, XML, or ZIP files for the export includes audio recordings) for varying compatibility with various analysis tools and software.

3.5 Offline and Remote Accessibility

Field linguistics often requires researchers to work in remote areas where internet infrastructure is lacking or entirely absent. In such environments, the reliance on a constant internet connection for data collection and analysis can severely hinder the progress of linguistic documentation efforts. Recognising this, one of the significant developments of the LangDoc system is the ability to operate effectively in both online and offline environments, which is crucial for uninterrupted linguistic data collection in remote field locations with sporadic or non-existent internet connectivity. A detailed explanation of the technical implementation, including data synchronisation, local storage, and system architecture will be presented in the following section.

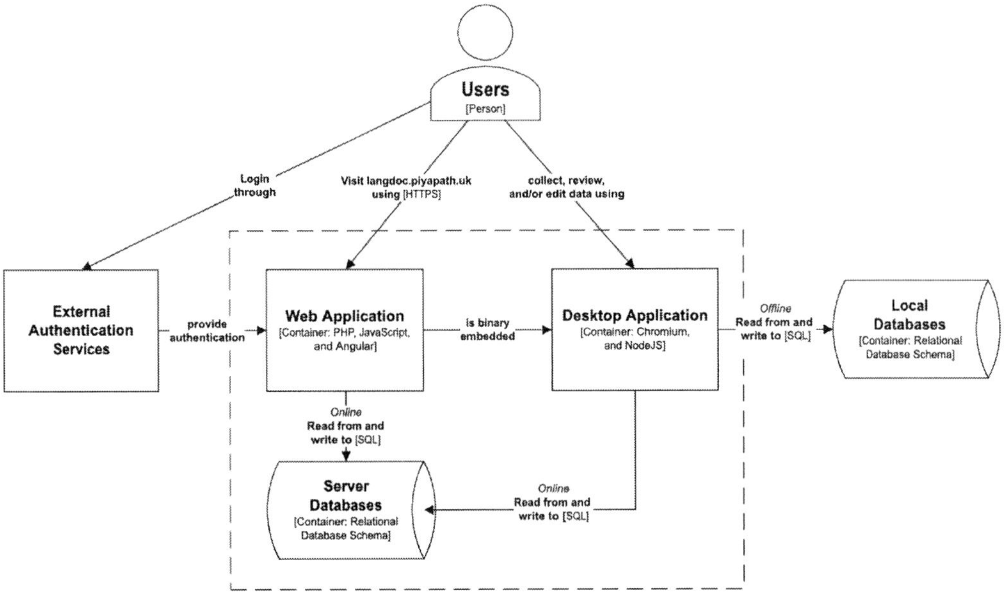

Figure 4: A high-level C4 container diagram of LangDoc system

3.6 System Architecture

As shown in Figure 4, LangDoc follows a client-server architecture with web-based user interfaces (i.e. web application and desktop application) interacting with a backend server that stores data in relational databases.

LangDoc supports external authentication methods, allowing users to authenticate using their accounts from external providers. This external authentication component communicates with the respective authentication providers' APIs to facilitate user login, registration, and account management.

The main interface for LangDoc is a web-based application. On the server-side, the application employs PHP to handle data processing, database interactions, and server-side logic, whilst Nginx web server is responsible for serving the application and handling HTTP requests. On the client-side, HTML, CSS, and JavaScript are used to create the user interface, handle user interactions, and provide a responsive and dynamic experience. The application also incorporate Angular, a JavaScript frameworks, to facilitate efficient development and maintainability. Though accessible on various devices, the interface is optimised for PC usage

LangDoc also offers the desktop interface designed specifically for offline word collection and temporary local storage, using an SQLite database to store linguistic data and project information. When the desktop application is online, it synchronises the locally stored data with the cloud database server. This process involves uploading any new or modified data to the server and downloading any updates or changes made by other users or collaborators. The desktop application is built using ChromiumOS rendering and Node.js for cross-platform compatibility, which allows for the creation of desktop applications using web technologies like HTML, CSS, and JavaScript to create a consistent user experience across systems.

The data synchronisation between the offline desktop application and the server is a crucial aspect of the LangDoc system. The mechanism adopts long-polling protocols to establish a connection between the desktop application and the cloud server. The desktop application stores data locally, keeping track of any new, modified, or deleted entries using timestamps during offline. It initiates the synchronisation process when detecting an internet connection. Timestamping is employed to prevent conflicts and determine which changes should take precedence, as the system allows multiple entries supported by the review system.

The deployment architecture of the LangDoc system varies depending on specific requirements and infrastructure available. For local development and testing purposes, the system is deployed on a virtual environment, with the web application running on Apache and the database server running on the same machine. For staging or production, the system is implemented on AWS cloud platform, hosted on an Canonical Ubuntu 22.04 E2 instance. The deployment architecture incorporates load balancing, caching, and optimisation techniques for scalability and availability. For security measures, SSL/TLS encryption and firewalls are implemented to protect the system and user data.

4 Evaluation and Case Study

It is always difficult to find a good matrix to measure the performance of software development systems such as LangDoc. However, evaluating its impact on language documentation projects is crucial for understanding its effectiveness and efficiency.

4.1 Comparative Analysis

To quantitatively evaluate the performance of LangDoc against traditional paper-based methods and computer-assisted audio recording, an experiment was conducted involving eight non-Vietnamese participants collecting Vietnamese vocabulary using the Swadesh-Yakhontov 35 wordlist across 3 different methods. Figure 5 visualises the central tendency distribution of time taken for each methods.

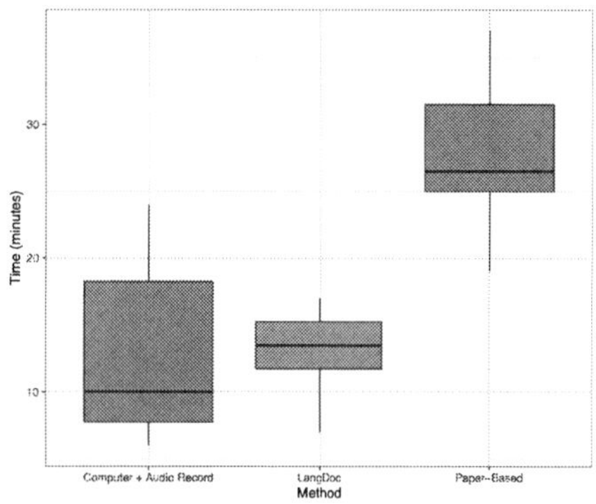

Figure 5: A boxplot of time taken for documenting tasks using different methods

One-way ANOVA showed a significant difference in mean times among methods ($F(2, 21)$ = 19.33, $p < 0.001$). Additionally, a post-hoc Tukey's HSD test indicated the paper-based method ($\bar{x}$ = 27.88, s = 5.59) took significantly longer than the computer with audio recording ($\bar{x}$ = 13.00, s = 7.03) and LangDoc ($\bar{x}$ = 13.13, s = 3.18) methods.

Overall, Figure 5 shows that both computer-assisted and LangDoc significantly improve data collection efficiency over paper-based methods, which, although gradually decreasing in modern fieldwork, still occur in certain scenarios. Besides, whilst traditional measure appears faster in median time, I argue that the consistency and accuracy of LangDoc's data collection process offer substantial long-term benefits by reducing the need for subsequent corrections and reverifications. Still, it is not appropriate to claim from the result as the experiment only involved the collection of 35 words and did not test the review process. Our case study on the Moklen language in the following section further demonstrates these advantages in a real-world setting.

4.2 Case Study: Documenting the Moklen Language

The case study of documenting the Moklen language in Phuket and Phang-nga, Thailand stands as evidence of LangDoc's effectiveness in addressing challenges faced by field linguists working with endangered languages and remote communities, as highlighted in the section 2.

Like many endangered languages, Moklen is predominantly spoken by the older generation, typically those above 50 years old who are Moklen-Thai bilingual (Pittayaporn and Choemprayong, Forthcoming). However, fluent speakers of the language are mostly amongst those exceeding 70 years old, restricting potential informants to only the elderly population. Despite their willingness to help teach the language and share knowledge, the documentation process itself can present unforeseen challenges due to the physical limitations that often come with age. Unlike younger generations having more stamina, extended recording sessions usually require elders to remain seated for longer periods. They may also need to repeat information or clarify pronunciations, which can be tiring. Additionally, the nature of documentation, where the duration are unstructured and depend on the flow of the conversation, is likely to inadvertently cause discomfort for elderly informants.

LangDoc's workflow and offline capabilities allowed researchers to conduct sessions at a comfortable pace for the elderly informants, reducing the chance of discomfort. The system facilitated the data collection process by preventing the clustering of records for words already documented. This feature not only accelerated the overall collection process but also minimised unnecessary post-processing tasks.

The ability to work offline and synchronise data

later proved invaluable, enabling researchers to focus on building rapport with informants. This led to more productive sessions and richer linguistic data collection. The motivation behind integrating offline functionality into LangDoc stems from the need to support fieldwork research in any setting, particularly for documenting endangered languages spoken by isolated communities like Moklen in Ko Phra Thong Island, Thailand. The offline capabilities allow greater flexibility, enabling researchers to collect data in the field and later synchronise it with central servers when internet access is restored, integrating into the broader project database.

Moreover, LangDoc's flexibility in both environment and wordlist configuration allowed the Moklen project to recollect sample audio recordings for each lemma, facilitating the production of a comprehensive Moklen dictionary. As of now, the Moklen language documentation project expects to compile a comprehensive database of over 1,000 words, complete with audio recordings, IPA transcriptions, and cultural annotations.

The success of the Moklen language documentation project underscores LangDoc's value in enhancing the efficacy and effectiveness of language documentation efforts, particularly in challenging field conditions. The system's ability to address the unique needs of endangered language communities and remote locations highlights its potential to support the documentation of linguistic diversity worldwide, preserving invaluable cultural heritage for future generations.

5 Discussion and Future Directions

The LangDoc system represents a step forward in optimising language documentation process, particularly for endangered languages in remote communities. However, it is essential to acknowledge the limitations of the current system. Whilst excelling in data collection and organisation, LangDoc primarily focuses on the preliminary stages of language documentation, currently limited to managing wordlists, transcriptions, and basic metadata. Additionally, the system's reliance on manual input and human involvement, even if mitigated through its collaborative features, may still introduce potential biases or inconsistencies, particularly in the transcription and annotation processes.

Integrating LangDoc with state-of-the-art NLP techniques could significantly enhance its capabilities to help linguists doing their works. For example, automated transcription and annotation tools could reduce manual effort and potential biases from humans, allowing linguists to provide essential oversight, control quality, and go further with analysis of complex linguistic phenomena beyond lexicons. Additionally, incorporating machine learning models trained on the collected data could assist in developing low-resource technologies, such as machine translation, parsing, and ASR systems for the documented languages.

Exploring ways to involve language communities more actively in the documentation process could foster a sense of ownership and promote the preservation of linguistic heritage. This could involve developing user-friendly interfaces for community members to contribute to data collection, validation, and dissemination efforts, in addition to the tool used solely by linguists.

6 Conclusion

This paper presented LangDoc as a system to address challenges in documenting endangered languages without standardised writing not only in the form of software tools but also via presenting logical steps for human workflow. By incorporating project management, wordlist-driven recording, collaborative review, and offline access, it improves documentation efficiency and quality. The Moklen case study demonstrated LangDoc's capabilities in tackling data duplication, verification bottlenecks, and accommodating elder informants. Whilst not a panacea, LangDoc streamlines workflows and enhances collaborative project effectiveness, helping preserve linguistic diversity and sustain endangered languages in its most foundational process.

Acknowledgments

The work would not be possible with out the help and participation of the Moklen community. I sincerely thanks Dr Pittayawat Pittayaporn for the opportunity to participate in his Moklen fieldwork (and this workshop deadline wake-up call). My gratitude extends to Dr Songphan Choemprayong for his endless support and critical comment on the near-final version. I also appreciate to my colleagues, Theera-anuchit Chalapinyo and Nichanan Pornsirivorarak, for their patience during the project's pilot period. Finally, I am grateful to three anonymous reviewers for their attentive reading of the paper and useful comments. Needless to say, only I am responsible for any remaining errors.

References

Steven Bird, Florian R. Hanke, Oliver Adams, and Haejoong Lee. 2014. Aikuma: A mobile app for collaborative language documentation. In *Proceedings of the 2014 Workshop on the Use of Computational Methods in the Study of Endangered Languages*, pages 1–5, Baltimore, Maryland, USA. Association for Computational Linguistics.

H. Andrew Black and Gary F. Simons. 2006. The SIL FieldWorks Language Explorer approach to morphological parsing. In *Proceedings of the 10th annual Texas Linguistics Society conference: Computational Linguistics for Less-Studied Languages*, pages 37–55, Austin, Texas, USA.

C. Browne, B. Culligan, , and J. Phillips. 2023. New general service list 1.2.

Bradley Wendell Compton. 2014. Ontology in information studies: without, within, and withal knowledge management. *Journal of Documentation*, 70:425–442.

Aharon B. Dolgopolsky. 1964. Gipoteza drevnejšego rodstva jazykovych semej severnoj evrazii s verojatnostej točky zrenija [a probabilistic hypothesis concering the oldest relationships among the language families of northern eurasia]. *Voprosy Jazykoznanija*, 2:53–63.

Aharon B. Dolgopolsky. 1986. A probabilistic hypothesis concerning the oldest relationships among the language families of northern eurasia. In Vitalij V. Shevoroshkin, editor, *Typology, relationship and time. A collection of papers on language change and relationship by Soviet linguists*, pages 27–50. Karoma Publisher, Ann Arbor. Originally published in 1964 as "Gipoteza drevnejšego rodstva jazykovych semej Severnoj Evrazii s verojatnostej točky zrenija" and translated from the Russian by V. V. Shevoroshkin.

Joel Robert William Dunham. 2014. *The online linguistic database: software for linguistic fieldwork*. Ph.D. thesis, The University of British Columbia.

Karen Emmorey and Harlan L. Lane. 2000. *The Signs of Language Revisited: An Anthology To Honor Ursula Bellugi and Edward Klima*. Psychology Press.

International Organization for Standardization. 2007. ISO 639-3:2007, Codes for the representation of names of languages – Part 3: Alpha-3 code for comprehensive coverage of languages.

James A. Matisoff. 1978. *Variational Semantics in Tibeto-Burman*. Institute for the Study of Human Issues.

Max Planck Institute for Psycholinguistics. 2023. ELAN (Version 6.7) [Computer software].

Sarah Moeller, Godfred Agyapong, Antti Arppe, Aditi Chaudhary, Shruti Rijhwani, Christopher Cox, Ryan Henke, Alexis Palmer, Daisy Rosenblum, and Lane Schwartz, editors. 2024. *Proceedings of the Seventh Workshop on the Use of Computational Methods in the Study of Endangered Languages*. Association for Computational Linguistics, St. Julians, Malta.

Pittayawat Pittayaporn and Songphan Choemprayong. Forthcoming. A proposal for a thai-based moklen orthography. *Language Documentation and Conservation*.

Jens Rasmussen and Kim J. Vicente. 1989. Coping with human errors through system design: implications for ecological interface design. *International Journal of Man-Machine Studies*, 31(5):517–534.

Keren Rice and Nicholas Thieberger. 2018. 225Tools and Technology for Language Documentation and Revitalization. In *The Oxford Handbook of Endangered Languages*. Oxford University Press.

Oleg Serikov, Ekaterina Voloshina, Anna Postnikova, Elena Klyachko, Ekaterina Vylomova, Tatiana Shavrina, Eric Le Ferrand, Valentin Malykh, Francis Tyers, Timofey Arkhangelskiy, and Vladislav Mikhailov, editors. 2023. *Proceedings of the Second Workshop on NLP Applications to Field Linguistics*. Association for Computational Linguistics, Dubrovnik, Croatia.

Sergej Starostin. 1991. *Altajskaja problema i proischoždenije japonskogo jazyka [The Altaic problem and the origin of the Japanese language]*. Nauka, Moscow.

Morris Swadesh. 1952. Lexico-statistic dating of prehistoric ethnic contacts. with special reference to north american indians and eskimos. *Proceedings of the American Philosophical Society*, 96(4):452–463.

Morris Swadesh. 1971. *The origin and diversification of language: Edited post mortem by Joel Sherzer*. Aldine, Chicago.

Daan van Esch, Ben Foley, and Nay San. 2019. Future directions in technological support for language documentation. In *Proceedings of the 3rd Workshop on the Use of Computational Methods in the Study of Endangered Languages Volume 1 (Papers)*, pages 14–22, Honolulu. Association for Computational Linguistics.

Søren Wichmann, Eric W. Holman, and Cecil H. Brown. 2007. Guidelines for preparing 40-word lists for languages to be included in the ajsp database. *The ASJP Database*.

Penwipa Yooyen. 2013. *Tone variation of Thai Song by age group in Ratchaburi province*. Ph.D. thesis, Mahidol University.

Ken Zook. 2024. *FLEx 9.1 Conceptual Model*. SIL International.

Leveraging Deep Learning to Shed Light on Tones of an Endangered Language: A Case Study of Moklen

Sireemas Maspong[1,2], Francesco Burroni[1,2], Teerawee Sukanchanon[2], Warunsiri Pornpottanamas[3], Pittayawat Pittayaporn[2]

[1]Spoken Language Processing Group, Institute for Phonetics and Speech Processing, LMU München
[2]Department of Linguistics & Center of Excellence in Southeast Asian Linguistics, Chulalongkorn University
[3]Department of English and Linguistics, Ramkhamhaeng University

Correspondence: s.maspong@phonetik.uni-muenchen.de

Abstract

Moklen, a tonal Austronesian language spoken in Thailand, exhibits two tones with unbalanced distributions. We employed machine learning techniques for time-series classification to investigate its acoustic properties. Our analysis reveals that a synergy between pitch and vowel quality is crucial for tone distinction, as the model trained with these features achieved the highest accuracy.

1 Introduction

Moklen, an endangered and understudied Austronesian language spoken along the western coast of southern Thailand (Larish, 2005), has sparked debate about its tonal status. While Austronesian languages are typically not tonal, Moklen exhibits a few minimal pairs suggesting the presence of two lexical tones (Larish, 1997; Pittayaporn et al., 2022).

The acoustic properties of Moklen tone were recently explored by Pornpottanamas et al. (2023). Their study revealed that Moklen tones are distinguished not only by pitch, but also by vowel quality and voice quality. Interestingly, these acoustic characteristics resemble those of register contrasts found in mainland Southeast Asian languages (Brunelle and Kirby, 2016). It is worth noting that the definition of tone in this paper refers to the suprasegmental contrast, which may be realized not only by pitch, but also by voice quality or vowel quality, similar to Vietnamese, Burmese, Shanghai Chinese, and other languages (See Abramson and Luangthongkum, 2009; Brunelle and Kirby, 2016).

What remains unclear is the relative weight of acoustic cues in Moklen tones and register systems. Phonetic contrasts often differ across multiple dimensions; for example, the English /b/ and /p/ differ in their voice onset time (VOT) as well as other dimensions, including the duration of stop closure and fundamental frequency (f0) after closure (Lisker, 1986). Furthermore, even though a contrast may involve several phonetic dimensions, they may not all be equally important. In other words, the phonetic cues may have different weights in production and/or perception. For instance, the English /b/ and /p/ are primarily distinguished by VOT, with f0 playing a secondary role (Abramson and Lisker, 1985). It is therefore possible that the acoustic cues in Moklen tones, including pitch, vowel quality, and voice quality, may have different relative weights.

In this paper, we investigate the contribution of individual acoustic features to Moklen tone distinction using an ablation study within a machine learning framework. We employed a Bidirectional Long Short-Term Memory (BiLSTM) Neural Network with self-attention for sequence classification. BiLSTM with self-attention has been used in tone recognition tasks in previous works (e.g., Yang et al., 2018). However, neural network classification has rarely been used with the tones of underrepresented languages such as Moklen.

This investigation confirms the presence of contrastive tones in Moklen. Furthermore, our analysis reveals that pitch and vowel quality features are crucial for distinguishing the two lexical tones. The model trained on this feature set achieved the highest accuracy in differentiating between Moklen tones.

1.1 Moklen and its lexical tones

Moklen is an indigenous language spoken by fewer than 4,000 people along the west coast of Phang Nga province in Thailand and on nearby islands (Arunotai, 2017). Currently, the language is facing endangerment, as its use is limited to older adults with low transmission to younger speakers (Pittayaporn et al., 2022).

Phonologically, Moklen shares similarities with mainland Southeast Asian (MSEA) languages, setting it apart from the broader insular Austronesian

Proceedings of the 3rd Workshop on NLP Applications to Field Linguistics (Field Matters 2024), pages 37–42
August 16, 2024 ©2024 Association for Computational Linguistics

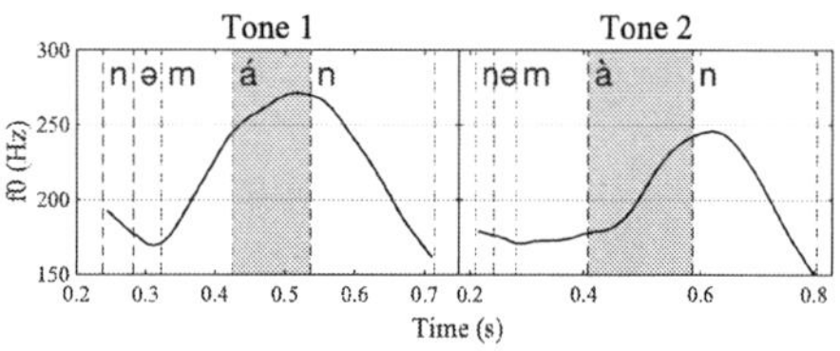

Figure 1: Difference in f0 of a minimal pair /nəmán/ 'to fish' *vs.* /nəmàn/ 'to be glad'.

Tone 1		Tone 2	
Words	**Glosses**	**Words**	**Glosses**
nəmán	'to fish'	nəmàn	'to be glad'
bəlá:	'to scold'	bəlà:	'dehusked rice'
nəmá:ʔ	'to enter'	dadà:ʔ	'breast'
ʔá:k	'to place'	ʔà:k	'crow'
namát	'wave, tide'	digàt	'bedbug'
kɔlá:t	'to be hot'	kɔlà:t	'mushroom'

Table 1: Examples of stimuli.

family (Larish, 1999; Pittayaporn, 2024). Two features relevant to this study, shared by Moklen and other MSEA languages, are systematic word-final stress and tonal contrast.

Moklen follows a consistent iambic stress pattern, with stress assigned to the last syllable of the foot (Larish, 1999; Swastham, 1982). Moklen tones are consistently realized only on the ultimate syllable, which also bears stress (Pittayaporn et al., 2022; Pornpottanamas et al., 2023). The two tones are not predictable from any phonological environments despite an unbalanced distribution: the majority of words carry Tone 1, while only about 10-20% carry Tone 2 (Larish, 1997). A few minimal pairs have been identified, as shown in Table 1.

Acoustically, the two tones differ in several ways. Tone 1 is generally higher-pitched compared to Tone 2, which has a lower pitch and a steeper rise on the stressed vowel (Figure 1). Additionally, Tone 1 vowels tend to be lower and slightly more front compared to Tone 2 vowels. Finally, Tone 2 exhibits breathiness, while Tone 1 is more modal. These acoustic properties remain consistent regardless of vowel length, onset voicing, or coda categories (Pornpottanamas et al., 2023).

While previous research has identified acoustic correlates of Moklen tones, including pitch, vowel quality, and voice quality, one question remains unanswered: the relative importance of these features in distinguishing the two lexical tones. It is unclear whether all features contribute equally or if a specific combination proves most effective. Investigating this question can provide deeper insights into the acoustic realization of Moklen tones and potentially contribute to the development of more efficient automatic speech recognition systems for Moklen.

1.2 Research questions

This paper investigates two key questions regarding Moklen tone:

(i) Can pitch, voice quality, and vowel quality features be used to distinguish the two Moklen tones?

(ii) Which combination of these acoustic features leads to the most accurate classification of Moklen tones?

2 Methodology

2.1 Data collection and processing

Eight native Moklen speakers from Phang Nga Province participated in this study. Four participants (3 females, 1 male) resided in Bang Sak village, while the remaining four (3 females, 1 male) resided in Lam Pi village. Although the participants are from two different villages, previous research has not observed dialectal differences between them (Pornpottanamas et al., 2023).

The participants ranged in age from 46 to 70 years old at the time of recording. Notably, all participants were bilingual in Moklen and Southern Thai, with Moklen being their dominant language.

The participants were instructed to produce Moklen monosyllabic and disyllabic words in isolation. The stimuli were presented orally in Thai, and participants were asked to translate them into Moklen. Each target word was repeated three times.

The stimuli consist of 98 attested Moklen words with stressed final syllables containing /a/ or /a:/ vowels. These target words were systematically varied in terms of tone, onset voicing, vowel length, and coda classes to achieve a balanced representation. Examples of the stimuli are provided in Table 1. Notably, there are 74 words with Tone 1 and 24 words with Tone 2. This unequal distribution of stimuli roughly reflects the actual proportion of these two tones within the Moklen lexicon. We did not control for the semantic or syntactic categories of the target words.

The recordings were manually segmented in Praat (Boersma and Weenink, 2020). From the stressed vowel intervals, five acoustic measurements were extracted to serve as time-series features in the classification process: fundamental frequency (f0) for pitch, first and second formant frequencies (F1, F2) characterizing vowel quality, the difference between corrected first harmonics and corrected spectral amplitude of F3 (H1*-A3*) (using the correction method from Iseli and Alwan, 2004), and Cepstral Peak Prominence (CPP) as measures of voice quality. These measurements are commonly reported as acoustic correlates of tone in Southeast Asian languages (Brunelle and Kirby, 2016). Measurements during the vowel interval were chosen over the rime (vowel and coda) interval because our target words include those with final voiceless stops. Many of these measurements, especially f0, F1, and F2, cannot be tracked during the voiceless stop coda interval. Therefore, measurements during the vowel interval provide the only fair comparison across all syllable structures.

PraatSauce (Kirby, 2018) was used to extract these acoustic measurements. A consistent window size of 30 milliseconds (ms) with a 5 ms time step was applied to all measurements. f0 tracking was performed in two steps to account for individual variations in f0 range across participants, following the method described in De Looze (2010).

To standardize the acoustic measurements, each participant's data were z-scored based on participant-specific mean and standard deviation.

2.2 Data preparation

To prepare the data for classification analysis, we first addressed missing values due to tracking errors using the fillmissing function in MATLAB (MathWorks, 2024), employing linear interpolation of neighboring, non-missing values. Trajectories with too few existing values that could not be adequately filled were removed. The remaining number of tokens for classification is 1,684 for Tone 1 and 567 for Tone 2.

We randomly partitioned the data into an 80:10:10 split for training, validation, and testing sets, respectively, using the cvpartition function in MATLAB. The training set contained 1,801 tokens (1,353 tokens of Tone 1 and 448 tokens of Tone 2), the validation set included 225 tokens (157 tokens of Tone 1 and 68 tokens of Tone 2), and the testing set comprised 225 tokens (174 tokens of Tone 1 and 51 tokens of Tone 2).

Due to the imbalanced class distribution, we upsampled Tone 2 tokens in the training set to match the number of Tone 1 tokens. To achieve a more robust classification, we augmented the training data using two methods adapted from Flores et al. (2021): time-warping and adding random Gaussian noise. We time-warped each token to a length randomly drawn from a Poisson distribution with a lambda parameter corresponding to the mean length of all tokens. Then, we added Gaussian noise with a standard deviation of 0.05 to all measurements of all tokens. Finally, we combined the permuted data with the original data to enlarge the training set. In total, our training set included 2,706 tokens for each tonal category.

Hyperparameters	Ranges	Optimized Values
# Hidden Layers	[1, 4]	1
# Hidden Units	[16, 64]	52
Batch Size	[16, 64]	23
Initial Learning Rate	[10^{-6}, 0.005]	0.0032

Table 2: Search ranges for Bayesian Optimization and the optimized values.

2.3 Sequence classification using bidirectional LSTM with Self-Attention

To classify Moklen tone, we trained a Bidirectional Recurrent Neural Network with Long Short-Term Memory units (BiLSTM). BiLSTM is well-suited for sequential tasks like speech recognition (Graves and Schmidhuber, 2005). Additionally, we enhanced the model by incorporating a self-attention mechanism to focus the network on the most relevant parts of the input sequence for tone classification.

The BiLSTM architecture consisted of an input layer with five units (one for each acoustic measurement), hidden layers using a sigmoid activation function, and an output layer with two units (one for each tone class), followed by a softmax layer for probability estimation. Additionally, recurrent dropout was applied to the hidden layer for regularization.

Other hyperparameters, including the number of hidden layers, number of hidden units, batch size, and initial learning rate, were optimized using Bayesian Optimization. The search ranges for Bayesian Optimization and the optimized values were summarized in Table 2.

2.4 Feature ablation

To assess the contribution of different acoustic feature sets to tone classification, we conducted a feature ablation study. We trained separate classification models with seven feature combination inputs:

	Features	Overall Acc.	Tone 1 Acc.	Tone 2 Acc.
(iii)	**Pitch+Vowel**	**84.0%**	**86.2%**	**76.5%**
(i)	Pitch+Voice+Vowel	81.3%	85.6%	66.7%
(v)	Pitch	79.6%	83.9%	64.7%
(ii)	Pitch+Voice	79.1%	83.3%	64.7%
(iv)	Voice+Vowel	78.2%	83.3%	60.8%
(vi)	Voice	73.3%	72.4%	62.7%
(vii)	Vowel	70.2%	77.6%	58.8%

Table 3: Accuracy of models with different feature combinations sorted based on the total accuracy.

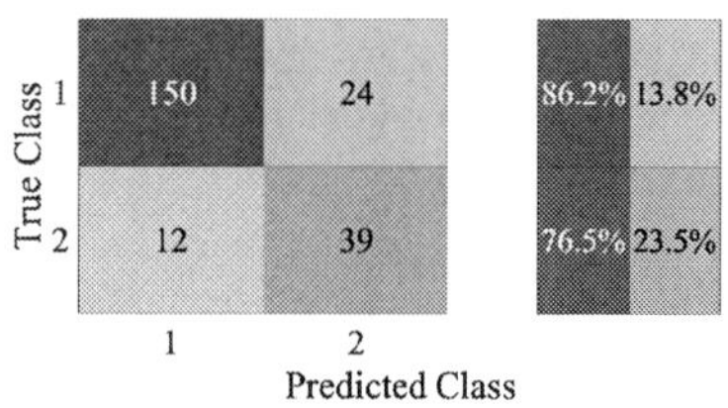

Figure 2: Confusion matrix of the model with pitch and vowel quality features.

(i) Pitch (f0), voice quality (CPP and H1*-A3*), and vowel quality (F1 and F2) features.
(ii) Pitch and voice quality features.
(iii) Pitch and vowel quality features.
(iv) Voice quality and vowel quality features.
(v) pitch features only.
(vi) Voice quality features only.
(vii) Vowel quality features only.

For a fair comparison across models, we applied the hyperparameters optimized using the model with all five feature inputs, as listed in (i), to all ablation models.

3 Results

3.1 Ablation study

We found that the performance of all models significantly exceeded the chance level (50% overall accuracy). Specifically, all models achieved an overall classification accuracy of over 70%, as shown in Table 3. The model using pitch (f0) and vowel quality (F1 and F2) features achieved the highest overall accuracy (84%) and F1-score (0.89). The confusion matrix of the model is illustrated in Figure 2. We also observed the importance of pitch information, as models excluding the pitch features exhibited lower performance, achieving the lowest accuracy among all models (Table 3).

An interesting observation is that the model using only pitch (f0) and vowel quality (F1 and F2) features exhibited significantly better performance

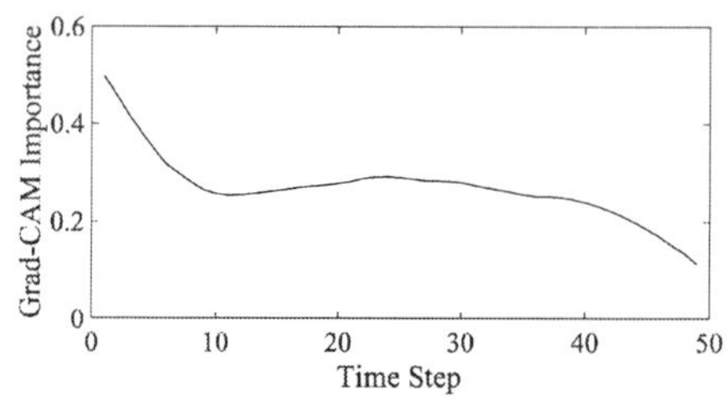

Figure 3: Grad-CAM importance map for a representative token classified by the best performing model.

in classifying Tone 2 tokens (76.5% accuracy) compared to other models (all below 70% accuracy for Tone 2). This behavior contrasts with the classification of Tone 1 tokens, where all models with pitch features performed similarly.

To understand which parts of the vowel trajectory contribute most to tone classification, we employed Gradient-weighted Class Activation Mapping (Grad-CAM) (Selvaraju et al., 2019). Figure 3 illustrates the Grad-CAM importance map for a representative token classified by our best-performing model. As evident from the map, the model focuses heavily on the vowel's onset, with the importance decreasing gradually towards the end. This observation aligns with the f0 trajectories presented in Figure 1, suggesting that the initial portion of the vowel plays a crucial role in distinguishing the tones.

3.2 Error analysis

We also conducted an error analysis on the best-performing model, (iii) Pitch + Vowel. We examined whether the following four features had an effect on the model's classification: onset voicing (voiced, voiceless), vowel length (short, long), coda manners of articulation (stop, nasal, fricative, glide, open syllable), and coda places of articulation (bilabial, alveolar, palatal, velar, glottal, open syllable).

To determine if any of these features affected the model's classification, we performed Chi-squared tests. Each feature was tested separately against the correct and incorrect classifications of the model as one of the variables.

Significant effects were observed for two features: vowel length ($\chi^2(1, 225) = 7.02, p = .008$) and coda places of articulation ($\chi^2(5, 225) = 14.82, p = .011$). The other two features did not show significant effects: onset voicing ($\chi^2(1, 225) = .33, p = .56$) and coda manners of articulation ($\chi^2(4, 225) = 8.46, p = .08$). These results suggest that vowel length and coda place of articulation significantly impacted the model's classification performance.

Regarding vowel length, it was found that words with long vowels were more likely to be misclassified than those with short vowels, with approximately 72% of the misclassified tokens being words with long vowels.

In terms of coda places of articulation, tokens with a velar coda were more frequently misclassified than those with other types of final consonants. Specifically, about 30% of tokens with velar codas were incorrectly classified, compared to only 12% of tokens with alveolar codas. Notably, none of the tokens with bilabial codas were misclassified.

We also examined whether unique words influenced the model's classification. However, no patterns were observed, leading us to conclude that unique words were not a direct factor in the model's errors.

4 Discussion and conclusion

Our investigation into Moklen tone classification using acoustic features sheds light on the nature of tones in this unique Austronesian language. The ablation study confirmed that all features (pitch, voice quality, and vowel quality) contribute to Moklen tone classification. This is evidenced by the findings that models utilizing only a single feature set representing each acoustic aspect achieved relatively good performance (> 70% accuracy). However, the model combining pitch and vowel quality achieved the highest overall accuracy and F1-score. This result suggests that a synergy between pitch and vowel quality information plays a crucial role in distinguishing the two Moklen tones.

One potential explanation for the importance of pitch and vowel quality in distinguishing Moklen tones lies in their historical development. As mentioned, tonal contrast in Moklen is an innovation absent in its ancestral language. Moklen tones may have developed from reanalyzing different contrasts, such as stress, that utilize pitch and vowel quality (Gordon and Roettger, 2017)

Furthermore, we observed that the models excluding the pitch features achieved the lowest accuracy. This finding confirms that pitch emerges as the primary cue for Moklen tone. On the other hand, although other acoustic cues can be used to distinguish the two Moklen tones, they appear to play a more secondary role.

Our analysis of the features' relative importance across time steps within the vowel interval revealed that the most important features cluster around the vowel onset. This suggests that the distinction between Tone 1 and Tone 2 is most salient at the onset of the vowel. This pattern closely aligns with register contrast, where the distinction between registers is most prominent at the vowel onset (Brunelle and Tạ, 2021).

We also conducted an error analysis on the best-performing model, examining four features: onset voicing, vowel length, coda manners, and coda places of articulation. Chi-squared tests revealed that vowel length and coda places of articulation significantly impacted the model's classification, with words having long vowels and velar codas being more frequently misclassified. Further investigation is needed to understand why vowel length and coda place of articulation affected the model's performance.

One potential aspect for future work is to investigate Moklen tones from the perspective of acoustic features within a larger time interval, such as the entire syllable rather than just the vowel interval used in this paper. In other words, there may be more aspects of the tones that we have not yet explored. This broader analysis could include features like the f0 peak location on the final open syllable or final syllable with sonorant coda, as shown in Figure 1, where Tone 1 generally exhibits an earlier peak compared to Tone 2.

Further investigation into the perception of the two tones by Moklen speakers could provide deeper insights into the nature of this unique tonal system.

This study demonstrates the potential of machine learning approaches for analyzing acoustic features in endangered languages like Moklen. By leveraging deep learning for tone classification, we can gain valuable insights into the sound system of a language, even with limited documentation or speaker availability. One limitation of Moklen tone documentation is that tones are not predictable from the phonological environment or comparative studies, making it challenging for language fieldworkers to identify tones in Moklen words. Classification models trained on words with identified tones can assist fieldworkers in identifying the tones of undocumented words. Furthermore, these models can aid in creating a dictionary of Moklen, which is an important step in language revitalization.

References

Arthur Abramson and Theraphan Luangthongkum. 2009. A fuzzy boundary between tone languages and voice-register languages. In G. Fant, H. Fujisaki, and J. Shen, editors, *Frontiers in phonetics and speech science*, pages 149–155. The Commercial Press, Beijing.

Arthur S. Abramson and Leigh Lisker. 1985. Relative power of cues: F0 shift versus voice timing. In Victoria A. Fromkin, editor, *Phonetic linguistics: Essays in honor of Peter Ladefoged*, pages 25–33. Academic Press, Orlando.

Narumon Arunotai. 2017. "Hopeless at sea, landless on shore": contextualising the sea nomads' dilemma in Thailand. *AAS working papers in social anthropology*, 31:1–27.

Paul Boersma and David Weenink. 2020. Praat: doing phonetics by computer.

Marc Brunelle and James Kirby. 2016. Tone and Phonation in Southeast Asian Languages. *Language and Linguistics Compass*, 10(4):191–207.

Marc Brunelle and Thành Tấn Tạ. 2021. Register in languages of Mainland Southeast Asia: the state of the art. In Paul Sidwell and Mathias Jenny, editors, *The languages and linguistics of Mainland Southeast Asia: A comprehensive guide*, pages 683–706. De Gruyter Mouton, Berlin/Boston.

Céline De Looze. 2010. *Analyse et interprétation de l'empan temporel des variations prosodiques en français et en Anglais*. Ph.D. Thesis, Université de Provence-Aix-Marseille I.

Anibal Flores, Hugo Tito-Chura, and Honorio Apaza-Alanoca. 2021. Data Augmentation for Short-Term Time Series Prediction with Deep Learning. In *Intelligent Computing*, pages 492–506, Cham. Springer International Publishing.

Matthew Gordon and Timo Roettger. 2017. Acoustic correlates of word stress: A cross-linguistic survey. *Linguistics Vanguard*, 3(1):20170007.

Alex Graves and Jürgen Schmidhuber. 2005. Framewise phoneme classification with bidirectional LSTM and other neural network architectures. *Neural Networks*, 18(5):602–610.

Markus Iseli and Abeer Alwan. 2004. An improved correction formula for the estimation of harmonic magnitudes and its application to open quotient estimation. In *2004 IEEE International Conference on Acoustics, Speech, and Signal Processing*, pages 669–672.

James P. Kirby. 2018. PraatSauce: Praat-based tools for spectral analysis.

Michael David Larish. 1999. *The position of Moken and Moklen within the Austronesian language family*. Ph.D. dissertation, University of Hawai'i at Manoa.

Micheal David Larish. 1997. Moklen-Moken Phonology: Mainland or Insular Southeast Asian Typology? In *Proceedings of the Seventh International Conference on Austronesian Linguistics*, pages 125–149, Leiden. Rodopi.

Micheal David Larish. 2005. Moken and Moklen. In K.A. Adelaar and N. Himmelmann, editors, *The Austronesian Languages of Asia and Madagascar*. Routledge.

Leigh Lisker. 1986. "Voicing" in English: A Catalogue of Acoustic Features Signaling /b/ Versus /p/ in Trochees. *Language and Speech*, 29(1):3–11. _eprint: https://doi.org/10.1177/002383098602900102.

MathWorks. 2024. MATLAB version: 24.1.0 (R2024a).

Pittayawat Pittayaporn. 2024. On Becoming Mainland: Unravelling Malay Influence on Moklenic Languages. *SOJOURN: Journal of Social Issues in Southeast Asia*, 3(1):62–89.

Pittayawat Pittayaporn, Warunsiri Pornpottanamas, and Daniel Loss, editors. 2022. *Moklen-Thai-English dictionary: a pilot version*. Academic Work Dissemination Project, Faculty of Arts, Chulalongkorn University, Bangkok.

Warunsiri Pornpottanamas, Sireemas Maspong, and Pittayawat Pittayaporn. 2023. A Preliminary Investigation of the Phonetic Characteristics of Moklen Tones. In *The Second International Conference on Tone and Intonation*, pages 59–63. ISCA.

Ramprasaath R. Selvaraju, Michael Cogswell, Abhishek Das, Ramakrishna Vedantam, Devi Parikh, and Dhruv Batra. 2019. Grad-CAM: Visual Explanations from Deep Networks via Gradient-Based Localization. *International Journal of Computer Vision*, 128(2):336–359. Publisher: Springer Science and Business Media LLC.

Pensiri Swastham. 1982. A description of Moklen: A Malayo-Polynesian language in Thailand. Master's thesis, Mahidol University.

Longfei Yang, Yanlu Xie, and Jinsong Zhang. 2018. Improving Mandarin Tone Recognition Using Convolutional Bidirectional Long Short-Term Memory with Attention. In *Proc. Interspeech 2018*, pages 352–356. ISSN: 2958-1796.

A Comparative Analysis of Speaker Diarization Models: Creating a Dataset for German Dialectal Speech

Lea Fischbach
Research Center Deutscher Sprachatlas
Marburg, Germany
Lea.Fischbach@uni-marburg.de

Abstract

Speaker diarization is a critical task in the field of computer science, aiming to assign timestamps and speaker labels to audio segments. The aim of these tests in this Publication is to find a pretrained speaker diarization pipeline capable of distinguishing dialectal speakers from each other and an explorer. To achieve this, three pipelines, namely Pyannote, CLEAVER and NeMo, are tested and compared, across various segmentation and parameterization strategies. The study considers multiple scenarios, such as the impact of threshold values for speaker recognition and overlap handling on classification accuracy. Additionally, this study aims to create a dataset for German dialect identification (DID) based on the findings from this research.

1 Introduction

Speaker diarization (SD) models are essential in various applications, including speech-to-text systems. Since existing SD systems may not always meet specific requirements, comparing multiple models is necessary to identify the most suitable one, aiding both our research and guiding other researchers.

The annual DIHARD Challenge, focusing on SD for challenging audio files, has been held since 2018 (Ryant et al., 2020). However, as demonstrated in this contribution to the Challenge (Horiguchi et al., 2021) and in an paper, which provides an overview of SD systems (Tranter and Reynolds, 2006), the commonly used evaluation metric is the one called diarization error rate (DER), based on False Alarm, Missed Detection, and Speaker Confusion. In our case this metric is not applicable due to the nature of our ground truth data. The recordings used are from the REDE corpus (Schmidt et al., 2020ff.), featuring 1-2 elderly male speakers translating sentences into their local dialect and an explorer providing this sentences beforehand in Standard German. Our manually segmented ground truth data only contains these translated sentences from the dialectal speaker, however the original recordings include additional utterances from the dialectal speaker, between these sentences, that we aim to retain. Using DER could distort results because the SD model might correctly identify an dialectal speaker during these intervals not captured in the ground truth data. Therefore, we bypass DER and use a dialectal classification model, comparing its accuracy on our manually segmented ground truth data (the resulting performance is our baseline) with the accuracy from the model on audio files created by the different SD pipelines. With clearly separated speakers, the recordings used for testing the model contain only the desired dialectal speaker and thus the model should perform better, because the explorer does not speak any dialect and thus would interfere with classification.

We utilize SD models including Pyannote (Bredin et al., 2020; Bredin and Laurent, 2021) (v2.1), CLEAVER[1], and NVIDIA NeMo (Harper et al.), highlighting their strengths, weaknesses, and key features. This comparative analysis provides valuable insights, saving researchers time and effort in selecting the most suitable model. The goal is to establish a dataset for German dialect identification (DID), advancing research in this field.

2 Overview

Speaker diarization (SD) is the task of assigning timestamps and corresponding speaker labels to an audio track. In general, pipelines designed to accomplish this task consist of four sub-tasks. Depending on the categorization and assignment, there can be even more sub-tasks, as seen in works such as (Tranter and Reynolds, 2006), where all

[1] https://www.oxfordwaveresearch.com/products/cleaver/

Proceedings of the 3rd Workshop on NLP Applications to Field Linguistics (Field Matters 2024), pages 43–51
August 16, 2024 ©2024 Association for Computational Linguistics

possible sub-tasks are analyzed, or in (Park et al., 2022) where pre- and post-processing also constitute sub-tasks.
The first of the four sub-tasks is Voice Activity Detection (VAD), which identifies when speech is present and removes non-speech sections from the audio. This is followed by segmentation, also known as Speaker Change Detection (SCD), which recognizes speaker transitions and divides the audio into individual speaker segments. Next, local speaker embeddings (SE) are extracted using a pretrained model. These embeddings are then utilized in a clustering algorithm, where speakers with similar embeddings are grouped together to label the speakers globally.

2.1 Pyannote

Pyannote is an open-source library built on PyTorch. There is a key difference between their model and many others: they use short audio chunks but with a higher temporal resolution of 16ms (Bredin and Laurent, 2021). This means that every 16ms, the model calculates the probability of each possible speaker being active. The use of shorter audio chunks plays a crucial role because they typically involve fewer speakers and exhibit less speaker variability, simplifying the task.
Another distinctive feature of Pyannote is its consideration of concurrent speakers. To account for this, a SE for an individual speaker is constructed only from the (concatenated) segments in which that speaker exclusively speaks. They refer to this approach as "overlap-aware" (Bredin, 2023). However, the accuracy of these segments depends on the primary segmentation task.

2.2 CLEAVER

Oxford Wave Research's CLEAVER (Cluster Estimation And Versatile Extraction of Regions) differs in that it utilizes phonetic features. For the SCD, it relies on pitch, which is extracted using Praat (Boersma and Weenink, 2023; Alexander and Forth, 2012). Whenever this pitch significantly deviates, either in time or frequency, a speaker change is detected, resulting in individual segments. Subsequently, using a statistical model, the most distinct segments are identified. These segments then undergo clustering, where all other segments are assigned to one of them. Following this, another clustering step takes place, where segments previous assigned to their respective speakers form the new start SE. This process continues until the clusters no longer change.

2.3 NeMo

NeMo (Neural Modules) is an open-source library developed by NVIDIA, built on PyTorch. This framework includes various tools in the field of Natural Language Processing. Its processes are optimized to work with a CUDA-compatible GPU[2]. Although NeMo is designed to be framework-agnostic, it currently supports only PyTorch as a backend.
A unique aspect of NeMo's SD pipeline is the inclusion of a "neural diarizer" after the clustering step[3]. This diarizer is applied to the speaker profiles obtained from clustering and is a trainable neural model. It assigns speaker labels even to overlapping speakers, which cannot be achieved with clustering alone. The process involves using a clustering diarizer to estimate the speakers profiles and the number of speakers by employing a pairwise (two-speaker) unit model for both training and inference.
Another advantage of NeMo is the concept of Multiscale Segmentation[3]. Normally, a speaker embedding (SE) is generated for each speaker segment. If long segments (over 3 seconds) are used, the speaker profile is reliable, but temporal information is lost since speaker changes can only be detected every 3 seconds. When short segments (0.5-3.0 seconds) are used, the speaker profile depends on a brief utterance by the speaker, making the SE unreliable. To address this issue, Multiscale Segmentation is employed. Segmentations of different lengths, which overlap, are utilized. For example, the audio is divided into segments of 0.5 seconds, 0.75 seconds, etc. Information from each segmentation is then combined and used for global speaker labels. Additionally, the smallest segmentation level is used as the temporal resolution, allowing the model to more accurately capture rapid changes in speaker activity.

3 Experimental Setup

In this section, we outline our experimental setup and the exploration of various parameters for our study. We analyze a total of 20 different Ger-

[2]https://docs.nvidia.com/deeplearning/nemo/user-guide/docs/en/stable/asr/speaker_diarization/intro.html

[3]https://github.com/NVIDIA/NeMo/blob/main/tutorials/speaker_tasks/Speaker_Diarization_Inference.ipynb

man dialects, classified according to Wiesinger (Wiesinger, 1983), amounting to 60.5 hours of audio data. Our focus narrows down to two specific dialects, contributing a combined 11.75 hours of audio, which are already annotated and clearly segmented, allowing them to serve as ground truth. We establish a baseline by assessing the model's accuracy on these manually segmented dialects.

The entire pipeline[4], from the normalization of the audios to obtaining the classification accuracy, is depicted in Figure 1. As a first step, all audio files undergo preprocessing to standardize their format. For this we chose a sample rate of of 16kHz driven by the requirements of Googles TRILLsson models (Shor and Venugopalan, 2022), where the largest model is employed for extracting feature embeddings. To extract feature embeddings, the audio segments resulting from Speaker diarization (SD) are concatenated per speaker and then divided into segments of 3 seconds each. These segments are then processed through a small convolutional neural network (CNN). The CNN model architecture comprises three dense layers with LeakyReLU activations and dropout layers to mitigate overfitting. For validating and testing the dialect classification model, we randomly selected two speakers from each dialect. Since the results vary depending on the chosen speakers, the steps of dividing the data into training, validation, and test sets and running the model are repeated 250 times, selecting new random speakers for each run. We then compute the mean accuracy out of these 250 runs. This number of runs has proven sufficient in previous tests to detect significant differences between experiments. For testing if the differences of the experiments are significant we use the Mann-Whitney U test (Mann and Whitney, 1947). We examine whether there is a significant difference between the baseline and the models accuracy using the resulting audios from various SD models with their default settings. Additionally, we evaluate whether there is a significant difference between runs using the resulting audios with the standard settings of each SD pipeline (called standard pipeline) and runs using the resulting audios with parameter adjustments for the SD pipelines or different segment extraction methods. This is indicated by the p-value in the tables, which always refers to the top row of each table. If the distribution of accuracy for the respective experiment is significantly better than that of the top row, the p-value is bolded.

Parameter adjustments are explained in the upcoming subsections for each SD pipeline, while extraction methods are tested in the same manner for each SD pipeline. In this context, an extraction method means specifying a threshold in seconds, where only the resulting segments of the SD pipeline longer than this threshold are retained. This threshold helps remove non-contiguous utterances, such as clearing one's throat, if they haven't already been eliminated by the SD pipeline. We then incrementally increase the threshold to assess whether the results improve or worsen.

3.1 Pyannote

To test Pyannote with different parameters and segment extraction methods, we only specify the number of speakers between 1 and 4 in the standard settings. We then compare these standard settings with various segment extraction methods, which consider only segments longer than a set threshold and remove overlapping segments where multiple speakers talk simultaneously. We also evaluate the model's performance when we specify the exact number of speakers, increase the speaker recognition threshold (SR-TH) to make the model more confident in classifying speakers, and set the `min_duration_off` parameter to 0, meaning no intra-speaker gaps are bridged.

3.2 CLEAVER

Since we used only the demo version of CLEAVER, different parameters cannot be tested. In this demo version, an audio file is uploaded to the server via an API, and a segment is selected for each occurring speaker in which only that speaker is active. The results are then presented visually and can be downloaded as a CSV file.

3.3 NeMo

NVIDIA NeMo provides three different configuration YAML files (a human-readable data format used for configuration), each created during model training with different recordings. Detailed information about the used parameters in the YAML files is available on their website[5]. The general YAML file is optimized for balanced performance across various domains. The meeting YAML file

[4] `https://github.com/WoLFi22/DialectClassificationPipeline`

[5] `https://docs.nvidia.com/deeplearning/nemo/user-guide/docs/en/main/asr/speaker_diarization/configs.html`

is designed for meetings with 3-5 speakers, and the telephonic YAML file is suited for telephone recordings involving 2-8 speakers, as stated in the comments in the corresponding YAML files. Parameters modified in the YAML files include `ignore_overlap` (whether overlapping speech is ignored), `oracle_num_speakers` (whether to use the exact number of speakers from the manifest file), and `min_duration_off` (the threshold for filling speech gaps within a speaker). This last parameter is akin to Pyannotes `min_duration_off` parameter. Other adjusted parameters include `onset` and `offset`. The onset parameter determines the threshold for identifying the start and end of speech segments, while the offset parameter determines the threshold for identifying the end of speech. Finally, `pad_onset` specifies the duration added before each speech segment.

4 Results

Table 1 presents the results of the standard pipelines (SP). The column *Avg. #Segments* refers to the average count of segments, assigned to the dialectal speaker after speaker diarization (SD), per original audio file. Similarly, *Avg. Sec.* represents the average duration of these segments. The column *Mean Accuracy* represents the average accuracy across 250 runs using different train/validation/test data splits.The SP of Pyannote, CLEAVER, and NeMo with the telephonic YAML file perform similarly well. CLEAVER generally extracts more segments than the other two models, but these segments are shorter on average. This is shown in Figure 2 (a), which displays a portion of a file with ground truth labels at the top and the labels of the respective SPs below, with overlapping segments shaded in gray. This figure also highlights that Pyannote is the only model by default that detects overlaps, though it struggles with identifying segments without speech.

NeMo with the telephonic YAML file initially yields the best results. Figure 2 (a) also shows that the segments from NeMo telephonic closely align with the ground truth segments. With the general YAML file, segments are often too long, as reflected in the higher average seconds shown in Table 1 and also visible in Figure 2 (a). The meeting YAML file improves this but still does not match the segmentation quality of the telephonic YAML file. This is likely because the used recordings resemble a telephone conversation, typically involving two speakers who occasionally overlap and speak in succession.

4.1 Pyannote

Specifying the exact number of speakers for segmentation with Pyannote makes little difference, as shown by the nearly identical values in the first and second rows of Table 2. Figure 2 (b) also shows that the segments of the three speakers are almost identical. However, a speaker was occasionally misclassified as another when we provided the exact number of speakers. Thus, providing the exact number of speakers seemed to confuse the model, and during clustering, more distant embeddings were assigned to the same speaker because of the predefined number of clusters.

Removing overlapping segments results in a slight, but not significant, improvement in accuracy. Without bridging intra-speaker gaps results in further subdividing previously connected segments. This leads to more segments of shorter duration, as indicated in Table 2 and shown in Figure 2 (b), but it does not significantly affect the classification models accuracy. When the speaker recognition threshold (SR-TH) is set to 0.8, a significant improvement in classification is observed. With this setting, embeddings are assigned to a speaker only when the model is more confident, resulting in better recognition of larger speaker gaps, as shown in Figure 2 (b).

4.2 CLEAVER

For CLEAVER we can only modify the segment extraction method. However, there is no significant difference between the results with different segment extraction thresholds, as shown in Table 3. The only observed difference is that segments become longer as the threshold increases, while the number of segments decreases accordingly.

4.3 NeMo

Specifying the exact number of speakers for the audio files makes little difference with NeMo (telephonic). This is evident in Figure 2 (c), where the segments from NeMo closely match those with the exact number of speakers, indicating that the speakers were already well recognized. When adding overlap, overlapping speakers are still not detected and the resulting segments are the same as before. The reason for this is unclear and cannot be determined at this time. When intra-speaker gaps are not filled, previously connected segments are further

subdivided, resulting in more segments on average with a shorter duration. However, this does not impact the accuracy of the classification model since the parameter is set to 0.2 by default for the telephonic YAML file, meaning only speaker gaps of 200ms are bridged. Reducing the parameter to 0.0 makes virtually no difference, as all segments of a speaker are concatenated for classification. The same applies to increasing the parameter to 0.5. When increasing the onset and corresponding offset thresholds for recognizing the start and end of speech segments, on average more but shorter segments are generated. As shown in Figure 2 (c), individual long segments are divided into multiple shorter segments as the threshold increases, aligning more closely with the ground truth data. Consequently, the mean accuracy significantly improves starting from a threshold of 0.5 for both parameters. Without padding on the onset, segments simply begin later, as clearly visible in Figure 2 (c). As a result, segments are shorter on average, and more segments are created since some segments are without padding no longer connected. However, this does not affect performance.
Regarding the segment extraction method, removing segments shorter than 0.5 to 1.0 seconds proves significantly better than the standard method, where all segments are retained. This improvement may be attributed to NeMo recognizing and labeling short speech segments, such as coughing or unclear brief expressions, which are filtered out with the extraction method.

5 Conclusion

This study investigated the performance of Speaker diarization (SD) models, Pyannote, CLEAVER, and NeMo, using various parameters and segmentation strategies. Our findings highlight the significant impact of model choice, segmentation method, and parameter settings on the accuracy and effectiveness of SD systems.
For our audio data and classification task, NeMo telephonic, using a higher threshold value of 0.5 for the onset and offset parameter and employing the extraction method that ignores segments shorter than 1.0 second, achieves the highest accuracy at 90.6%. The baseline, composed of manually segmented recordings, achieves a slightly higher accuracy of 91.4%. Achieving baseline accuracy through automatic segmentation based solely on SD poses challenges in our case, because manually segmented recordings contain only relevant dialectal speech, while automatically generated ones also include free, sometimes Standard German, speech by dialectal speakers.
Although NeMo performs slightly better than Pyannote, where segments shorter than 0.5 seconds were ignored or the speaker recognition threshold (SR-TH) was increased, the difference is not substantial. Generally, however, it can be said that thanks to the concept of multiscale segmentation, NeMo also identifies shorter segments that are no longer recognized by Pyannote. Removing shorter segments resulting from speaker diarization, typically less than one second in duration, consistently improved accuracy. These segments are likely too short to contain coherent utterances from one speaker and instead often include background noise or filler words.
Since CLEAVER performs similarly well to Pyannote and NeMo without further adjustments, CLEAVER is a good alternative for those who prefer a visual representation.
It is also important to consider that perfect segmentation is not always necessary for practical purposes. Higher accuracy is of course better, but even slightly less accurate segmentation can still save time compared to manual segmentation. When adjusting the speaker recognition thresholds and the thresholds for identifying the start and end of speech segments, a balance must be struck between capturing every part of the audio where the desired speaker speaks (accepting more noise and larger speaker pauses or occasional misidentified speakers) and achieving higher precision (potentially missing some parts of the speakers speech and failing to assign some segments to the correct speaker).
With these insights, recordings from the REDE corpus can now be processed to create a new dataset for German dialect classification.

Acknowledgements

This research is supported by the Academy of Science and Literature Mainz (grant REDE 0404), the Federal Ministry of Education and Research of Germany (BMBF) (grant AnDy), and the Research Center Deutscher Sprachatlas in Marburg. Furthermore, thanks are due to Oxford Wave Research Ltd for granting access to the demo version of CLEAVER.

References

Anil Alexander and Oscar Forth. 2012. Blind speaker clustering using phonetic and spectral features in simulated and realistic police interviews.

Paul Boersma and David Weenink. 2023. Praat: doing phonetics by computer [Computer program]. http://www.praat.org/.

Hervé Bredin. 2023. pyannote.audio 2.1 speaker diarization pipeline: principle, benchmark, and recipe. *INTERSPEECH 2023*.

Hervé Bredin and Antoine Laurent. 2021. End-to-end speaker segmentation for overlap-aware resegmentation. pages 3111–3115.

Hervé Bredin, Ruiqing Yin, Juan Manuel Coria, Gregory Gelly, Pavel Korshunov, Marvin Lavechin, Diego Fustes, Hadrien Titeux, Wassim Bouaziz, and Marie-Philippe Gill. 2020. Pyannote.audio: Neural building blocks for speaker diarization. In *ICASSP 2020 - 2020 IEEE International Conference on Acoustics, Speech and Signal Processing (ICASSP)*, pages 7124–7128.

Eric Harper, Somshubra Majumdar, Oleksii Kuchaiev, Li Jason, Yang Zhang, Evelina Bakhturina, Vahid Noroozi, Sandeep Subramanian, Koluguri Nithin, Huang Jocelyn, Fei Jia, Jagadeesh Balam, Xuesong Yang, Micha Livne, Yi Dong, Sean Naren, and Boris Ginsburg. NeMo: a toolkit for Conversational AI and Large Language Models.

Shota Horiguchi, Nelson Yalta, Paola Garcia, Yuki Takashima, Yawen Xue, Desh Raj, Zili Huang, Yusuke Fujita, Shinji Watanabe, and Sanjeev Khudanpur. 2021. The hitachi-jhu dihard iii system: Competitive end-to-end neural diarization and x-vector clustering systems combined by dover-lap. *Preprint*, arXiv:2102.01363.

H. B. Mann and D. R. Whitney. 1947. On a Test of Whether one of Two Random Variables is Stochastically Larger than the Other. *The Annals of Mathematical Statistics*, 18(1):50 - 60.

Tae Jin Park, Naoyuki Kanda, Dimitrios Dimitriadis, Kyu J. Han, Shinji Watanabe, and Shrikanth Narayanan. 2022. A review of speaker diarization: Recent advances with deep learning. *Computer Speech & Language*, 72:101317.

Neville Ryant, Kenneth Church, Christopher Cieri, Jun Du, Sriram Ganapathy, and Mark Liberman. 2020. Third dihard challenge evaluation plan. *arXiv preprint arXiv:2006.05815*.

Jürgen Erich Schmidt, Joachim Herrgen, Roland Kehrein, and Alfred Lameli. 2020ff. Regionalsprache.de (REDE III). Forschungsplattform zu den modernen Regionalsprachen des Deutschen. Marburg: Forschungszentrum Deutscher Sprachatlas.

Joel Shor and Subhashini Venugopalan. 2022. TRILLsson: Distilled Universal Paralinguistic Speech Representations. In *Proc. Interspeech 2022*, pages 356–360.

S.E. Tranter and D.A. Reynolds. 2006. An overview of automatic speaker diarization systems. *IEEE Transactions on Audio, Speech, and Language Processing*, 14(5):1557–1565.

Peter Wiesinger. 1983. Die einteilung der deutschen dialekte. In Werner Besch, editor, *Dialektologie: Ein Handbuch zur deutschen und allgemeinen Dialektforschung*, volume 1.2 of *Handbücher zur Sprach- und Kommunikationswissenschaft*, pages 807–900. Berlin/New York: de Gruyter, Berlin, New York.

A Appendix

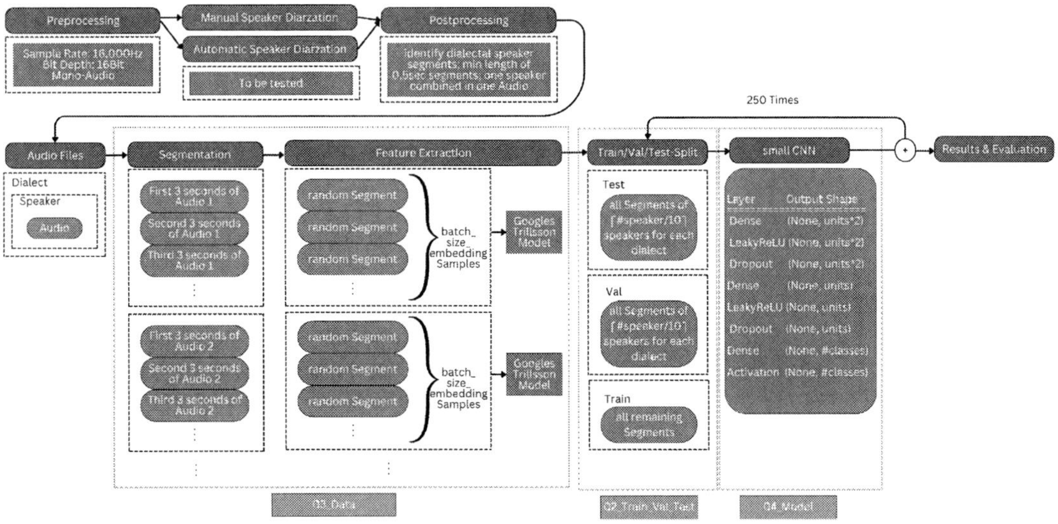

Figure 1: Visualization of used Pipeline

Model	Avg. #Segments	Avg. Time	Mean Accuracy
Baseline	85.257	1.974s	0.914
Pyannote	132.923	2.907s	0.878
CLEAVER	178.553	1.497s	0.877
NeMo general	139.205	3.251s	0.862
NeMo meeting	138.231	2.873s	0.867
NeMo telephonic	206.077	1.688s	0.880

Table 1: Results of standard pipelines

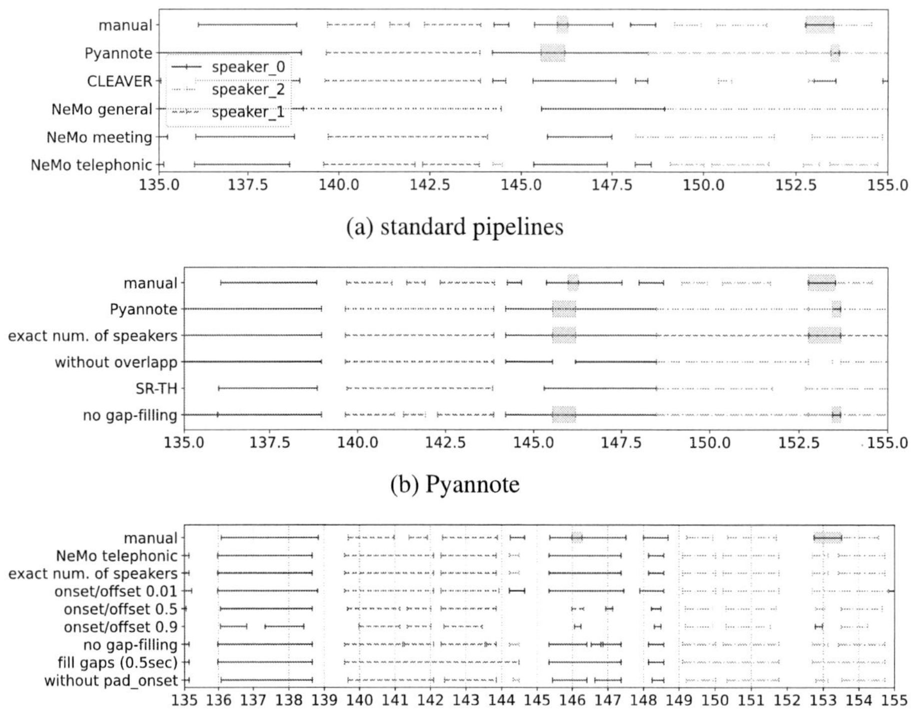

(a) standard pipelines

(b) Pyannote

(c) NeMo

Figure 2: Part of one Audio visualized after speaker diarization for the different models and parameters.

Params	Extract. Method	Avg. #Segments	Avg. Time	Mean Acc.	p-value
SP	-	132.923	2.907s	0.878	-
exact num. of speakers	-	132.87	2.85s	0.882	0.28
-	0.2sec.	130.10	2.97s	0.888	0.11
-	0.5sec.	123.33	3.12s	**0.889**	**0.05**
-	1.0sec.	111.33	3.35s	0.884	0.20
-	without overlap	134.31	2.64s	0.877	0.74
no gap-filling	-	167.49	2.30s	0.874	0.61
SR-TH 0.8	-	140.31	2.39s	**0.890**	**0.01**
SR-TH 0.8	0.5sec	126.28	2.60s	**0.890**	**0.02**

Table 2: Results from Pyannote

Params	Extract. Method	Avg. #Segments	Avg. Time	Mean Acc.	p-value
SP	-	178.553	1.497s	0.877	-
-	0.2sec.	162.97	1.62s	0.885	0.74
-	0.5sec.	134.13	1.88s	0.880	0.79
-	1.0sec.	101.74	2.21s	0.881	0.25

Table 3: Results from CLEAVER

Params	Extract. Method	Avg. #Segments	Avg. Time	Mean Acc.	p-value
SP (telephonic)	-	206.077	1.688s	0.880	-
exact num. of speakers	-	207.39	1.70s	0.879	0.44
-	0.2sec.	204.41	1.70s	0.882	0.24
-	0.5sec.	184.13	1.83s	**0.893**	**0.04**
-	1.0sec.	133.62	2.18s	**0.894**	**0.01**
-	1.5sec.	95.03	2.52s	0.883	0.19
with overlap	-	206.08	1.69s	0.880	0.38
onset/offset 0.01	-	185.59	1.99s	0.882	0.31
onset/offset 0.5	-	239.67	1.24s	**0.902**	**0.00**
onset/offset 0.9	-	300.82	0.76s	**0.891**	**0.00**
no gap-filling	-	257.13	1.35s	0.884	0.13
fill gaps (0.5sec)	-	163.21	2.26s	0.873	0.88
without pad_onset	-	230.31	1.41s	0.889	0.05
onset/offset 0.5	1.0sec.	112.28	1.87s	**0.906**	**0.00**

Table 4: Results from NeMo (telephonic)

Noise Be Gone: Does Speech Enhancement Distort Linguistic Nuances?

Iñigo Parra
The University of Alabama*
Tuscaloosa, AL
iparra@berkeley.edu

Abstract

This study evaluates the impact of speech enhancement (SE) techniques on linguistic research, focusing on their ability to maintain essential acoustic characteristics in enhanced audio without introducing significant artifacts. Through a sociophonetic analysis of Peninsular and Peruvian Spanish speakers, using both original and enhanced recordings, we demonstrate that SE effectively preserves critical speech nuances such as voicing and vowel quality. This supports the use of SE in improving the quality of speech samples. This study marks an initial effort to assess SE's reliability in language studies and proposes a methodology for enhancing low-quality audio corpora of under-resourced languages.

1 Introduction

Speech is a fundamental mode of human communication, consisting primarily of two components: speech production and speech perception (Deller Jr et al., 1993). Speech production enables individuals to articulate ideas through sound using linguistic structures. Conversely, speech perception involves the decoding of sound waves generated during speech production. These processes can be influenced by external factors such as ambient or background noise, potentially disrupting the communication sequence (Michelsanti et al., 2021).

Humans have evolved mechanisms to filter out these disturbances (Bronkhorst, 2000; Cherry, 1953; Shinn-Cunningham and Best, 2008). However, audio recordings capture both desired and undesired signals indiscriminately. This poses significant challenges for sociophonetic research, which often relies on pre-recorded audio data. Speech enhancement (SE) techniques clean and filter these recordings from external noise, thus enhancing the perceptual quality of the speech (Michelsanti et al., 2021). This presents SE as a useful tool for refining audio corpora.

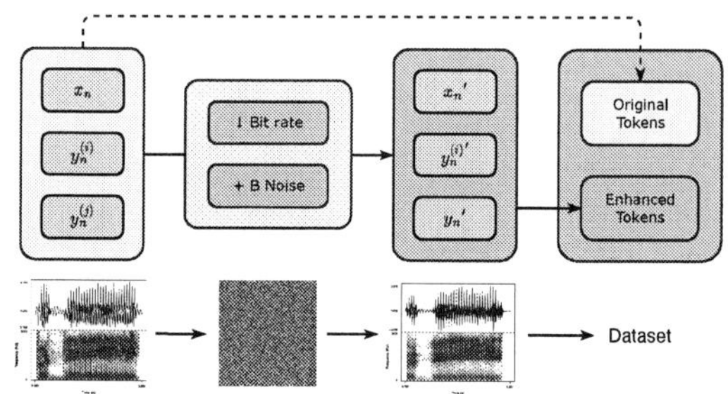

Figure 1: Diagram of the token processing. x_n represent intervocalic voiceless fricative tokens (e.g., /asa/); $y_n^{(i)}$ and $y_n^{(j)}$ represent vocalic /e/ (e.g., /bre/) and /i/ (e.g., /li/) tokens respectively. The original tokens are copied. One version is stored in the final dataset, while the other is processed as explained above to provide the enhanced copies $y_n^{(i)'}$ and $y_n^{(j)'}$. The final dataset includes all tokens, original and enhanced.

The reliability of speech enhancement models in improving the quality of linguistic speech corpora remains an open question. Sociophonetic studies, which explore speech variations among different social groups, provide a robust framework for testing SE models to ensure they maintain essential acoustic characteristics (e.g., vowel quality or voicing). Moreover, these methodologies often focus on subtle speech variations, making them ideal for assessing the ability of SE models to retain these nuances post-enhancement.

This study seeks to evaluate the effects of SE on linguistic corpora by conducting paired sociophonetic studies. We present a case study that examines the voicing and duration of intervocalic voiceless fricatives, as well as vocalic quality variations between Peninsular and Peruvian Spanish speakers. Our findings indicate that the studies using original and enhanced recordings yield comparable results. To our knowledge, this is the first work (1) *address-*

*Current affiliation: UC Berkeley, Department of Linguistics, Berkeley, CA.

Proceedings of the 3rd Workshop on NLP Applications to Field Linguistics (Field Matters 2024), pages 52–60
August 16, 2024 ©2024 Association for Computational Linguistics

ing such questions from a linguistic viewpoint and (2) *proposing a novel methodological approach for handling low-quality audio data in linguistic studies*.

2 Previous Work

Although there is ongoing research into the bias introduced by enhanced recordings (Isik et al., 2020), the linguistic community continues to debate the risk of distorting results through potential artifact introduction during enhancement. Previous technologies like WaveNet (Van Den Oord et al., 2016) have shown the ability to replicate speech with particular linguistic and acoustic subtleties (Chen et al., 2018); however, further exploration in this area is limited.

Most of the sociophonetics studies dealing with technology have focused on audio quality. Calder et al. (2022) studied the usability of Zoom as a tool for recording speech data. They found that F1 and F2 values showed significant differences compared to speech recorded with specialized equipment. Rathcke et al. (2017) look at how different normalization methods affect recordings with different degrees of quality, showing that normalization procedures may be relevant to address technical factors in low-quality recordings. Background noise has also been a central topic for perceptual studies, which coincide in that it should be eliminated as much as possible (Thomas, 2002, 2013). To this issue, filtering (Gradoville et al., 2022), especially low-pass, may be useful; however, there is a risk of deleting relevant nuances of speech production. Overall, while some works have used methodologies borrowed from linguistics (Michelsanti et al., 2021), SE has not had much attention in the field.

Avoiding hard filtering is crucial to analyzing high-frequencies (HF) content-heavy speech. Studies have gradually recognized the importance of retaining HF content in speech signals (Best et al., 2005; Yu et al., 2014), particularly when analyzing fricatives (Kharlamov et al., 2023; Jacewicz et al., 2023). Fricatives, which are rich in high-frequency energy, have shown to play a significant role in distinguishing phonetic and phonological features (Jongman et al., 2000). In the context of Peruvian Spanish and Peninsular Spanish, analyzing the voicing of fricatives before and after enhancement is particularly insightful. Chládková et al. (2011) offered a detailed description of Peruvian and Peninsular Spanish and Morrison et al. (2007) compared vocalic sounds in both variations, showing that Peruvian speakers reproduced higher fundamental frequency values.

3 Methodology

3.1 Data

We use two sources of data. The Peruvian Spanish tokens are extracted from a crowd-sourced Latin American Spanish dataset (Guevara-Rukoz et al., 2020), which included recordings of speakers from Lima. The Peninsular Spanish tokens were extracted from an open-source speech corpus from Kaggle (Fonseca, 2023) containing recordings of speakers from Madrid. Both datasets included short recordings (5-10s) of middle-class male and female speakers. We selected eight speakers, divided into two equal groups per variation. We did not consider the education level for this study[1].

From the recording pool of each speaker, we filtered those containing vowels /e/ and /i/, as well as fricative voiceless /s/ in intervocalic contexts. We then filtered out the tokens containing pre-vocalic nasals since they potentially reduce the acoustic power of the sound due to the introduction of antiresonances in the spectrum (Vampola et al., 2020). Sounds /i/ and /e/ have already been studied due to their alternations in Spanish (Brame and Bordelois, 1973). Because they share features (both are front vowels) and diverge in tongue height, any applied enhancement should be able to preserve the unique characteristics of each sound.

The total original tokens for both Spanish variants are described in Table 1. The number of enhanced tokens is the same as the ones described below; therefore, the study analyzed $N = 208$ tokens (for more details, see Appendix B).

Type	Total (n)	/s/ v_v			/i/			/e/		
		Total	M	F	Total	M	F	Total	M	F
Peruvian	68	14	7	7	25	15	10	29	14	15
Peninsular	70	14	7	7	29	14	15	27	13	14

Table 1: Descriptive statistics of the original tokens. With the enhanced tokens, the amount is doubled.

3.2 Token Enhancement

After duplicating the original tokens, we designed a perturbation function that applies additive white

[1] https://github.com/IParraMartin/A2A-ACL24

Model	Coefficient	Estimate	Std. Error	t value	p value	Estimate	Std. Error	t value	p value
Voicing	(Intercept)	4.994	2.057	2.427	**.022**	4.172	1.938	2.152	**.041**
	countrySpain	1.564	2.376	.658	.5163	2.488	2.238	1.112	.276
	genderM	.257	2.376	.108	.914	.015	2.238	.007	.994
Duration	(Intercept)	-4.584	.006	-694.89	**<.01**	-4.584	.006	-714.586	**<.01**
	countrySpain	-.022	.007	-3.00	**<.01**	-.020	.007	-2.796	**<.01**
	genderM	-.005	.007	-.75	0.46	-.006	.007	-.868	.393

Table 2: Results from the generalized linear models (GLM) for voicing and duration using original (left) and speech-enhanced tokens (right).

Gaussian noise (AWGN) to the copies (see Appendix A). We then blended the noise in the background and decreased the bit rate of the sound. To restore the sound, we use Voicefixer (Liu et al., 2021), a neural vocoder-based audio-to-audio model.

3.3 Voicing Experiments: Intervocalic Fricative /s/

In the intervocalic /s/ voicing experiments, we looked for segment voicing variations among the original and enhanced tokens. We fitted multiple statistical models to analyze both versions: ANOVAs, generalized linear models (GLM), robust linear models (RLM), and robust linear mixed-effects models (RLMEM). After analyzing conditions separately, we fit two additional models using condition as a predictor (IV) of voicing and duration (DV) (Appendix C).

The selection of diverse models was motivated by the practices in linguistics literature and the specific characteristics of our data. Although ANOVAs are widely used in linguistic research, we encountered issues related to the robustness of their results with our data specifications. To address these concerns, we tested robust models (RLM and RLMEM) that offer more flexibility in handling data assumptions. Additionally, GLMs were used, providing reliability and reinforcing our findings compared to other methods. This comprehensive approach ensures a robust examination of the variables under study.

3.4 Vocalic Quality Experiments: /i/ vs /e/

To account for the changes in the vocalic quality of /i/ and /e/ tokens, we conducted principal component analyses (PCA) and Procrustes analyses before and after enhancement. We examine the measurements of the first (F1) and second (F2) formant values at 16 evenly spaced intervals throughout the duration of vocalic tokens. These measurements form n-dimensional arrays that we call F-vectors. We compare these F-vectors using PCA and Procrustes tests to assess the statistical significance of the quality changes observed between the original and processed audio tokens.

4 Results

4.1 Voicing of Fricative /s/

Paired Experiments

In Table 2, we provide the results for the models with the best fits during paired experimentation.

In terms of voicing, there was a significant positive effect in the model's intercept using the original tokens ($\beta = 4.994, p = .02$) and the one using enhanced versions ($\beta = 4.172, p = .041$). This indicates that the baseline level of the response variable is significantly different from zero when all other predictors are held constant. However, based on the pseudo-R^2 metrics (ρ), these results show weak effect sizes ($\rho = .01$ and $\rho = .04$ respectively). For voicing, the effects attributed to being Peninsular or being male were not statistically significant. The effect of gender and location was negligible across both models, with high p-values, suggesting that they do not influence voicing in intervocalic fricatives when comparing Peninsular and Peruvian Spanish.

When examining duration, there was a significant negative effect in the intercepts of both models. We also found that the intercepts were identical for the model using the original tokens and the one using their processed versions ($\beta = -4.584, p < .01$). Interestingly, being Peninsular was a significant predictor of duration ($p < .01$), and it was associated with a decrease in the frication ($\beta = -.022$). This result was also reflected in the model using SE tokens ($\beta = -.020, p < .01$). Unlike voicing, the results for duration also showed high effect sizes, $\rho = .28$ and $\rho = .25$ for SE tokens, which are considered to show excellent model fits (McFadden, 1972).

Analyzing the results for voicing and duration in intervocalic /s/ when comparing paired models, we found no evidence suggesting that the enhanced tokens significantly modified or contaminated the original audio samples.

Interaction Experiments

In Table 3, we provide the results of generalized linear models using condition (original or enhanced) as an independent variable.

Model	Coefficient	Estimate	Std. Error	t value	p value
Voicing	(Intercept)	4.977	1.797	**2.769**	**<.01**
	countrySpain	.757	2.273	.333	.74
	genderM	-1.132	2.273	-.498	.62
	conditionOG	.48	1.607	.299	.766
	countrySpain:genderM	2.537	3.215	.789	.433
Duration	(Intercept)	-4.595	.004	**-993.02**	**<.01**
	countrySpain	.001	.005	.244	.808
	genderM	.017	.005	**2.928**	**<.01**
	conditionOG	-.001	.004	-.259	.796
	countrySpain:genderM	-.046	.008	**-5.608**	**<.01**

Table 3: Results from the generalized linear models (GLM) for voicing and duration using condition as independent variable. Underlined results show no significant impact of the condition on voicing and duration of intervocalic fricative (s). OG stands for original.

The generalized linear model for voicing demonstrated a significant intercept ($\beta = 4.977, p < .01$), indicating that the baseline level of voicing is significantly different from zero when all other predictors are controlled. However, the effects of being from Spain ($\beta = .757, p = .740$), being male ($\beta = -1.132, p = .620$), and the condition of original tokens ($\beta = .48, p = .766$) were not statistically significant. The interaction between being from Spain and being male ($\beta = 2.537, p = .433$) also showed no significant impact on voicing. The model accounted for a small portion of the variance in voicing, with a pseudo-R^2 value of $\rho = .043$.

In contrast, the model for duration revealed more significant effects. The intercept was significant and negative ($\beta = -4.595, p < .01$), suggesting a strong baseline effect on duration. The effect of gender was significant, with males exhibiting longer duration ($\beta = .017, p < .01$). The condition of the original tokens did not significantly influence duration ($\beta = -.001, p = .796$). Notably, the interaction term for being a male from Spain indicated a substantial negative impact on duration ($\beta = -.046, p < .01$). The models for duration displayed excellent fit, with pseudo-R^2 values of $\rho = .546$ for both original and enhanced tokens, indicating robust explanatory power.

These results highlight the differing effects of demographic factors and experimental conditions on voicing and duration. While factors such as gender significantly influenced duration, they had minimal effects on voicing. As for condition, the experimental manipulation of audio enhancement did not significantly alter the outcomes, indicating robustness in preserving phonetic characteristics. All these results seem to reflect that the nuanced properties of audio are preserved after SE.

4.2 Vocalic Quality

In this section, we compare the results of the vocalic quality of the Peninsular and Peruvian variants before and after audio enhancement.

/e/ Sound

This section presents the results of the Procrustes analysis performed to compare the principal component analyses (PCA) of the original and enhanced /e/ vocalic sounds across the different demographic groups (Figure 2).

For Peninsular Spanish speakers, the Procrustes analysis revealed distinctive outcomes based on gender. Female speakers demonstrated a Procrustes Sum of Squares (M_{12}) of .121, indicating a moderate degree of shape difference between the original and enhanced datasets. Despite this, a high correlation in a symmetric Procrustes rotation (.937) suggested that the overall structural integrity of the vowel space was largely maintained ($p < .01$). In contrast, male speakers displayed lower Procrustes ($M_{12} = .04$), showing closer alignment between the original and enhanced forms. The correlation coefficient was significantly high (.979), indicating an effective preservation of acoustic characteristics after enhancement. These results were also statistically significant ($p < .01$).

The results for Peruvian Spanish speakers further emphasized the effectiveness of speech enhancement techniques. Female speakers showed an even smaller deviation between the original and enhanced datasets ($M_{12} = .03$). The correlation coefficient (.984) reflected the preservation of vowel characteristics post-enhancement, with a statistically significant value ($p < .01$). Male speakers exhibited $M_{12} = .031$, with a correlation of .984. These results suggest that the speech enhancement process robustly maintained the integrity of the vocalic sounds ($p < .01$).

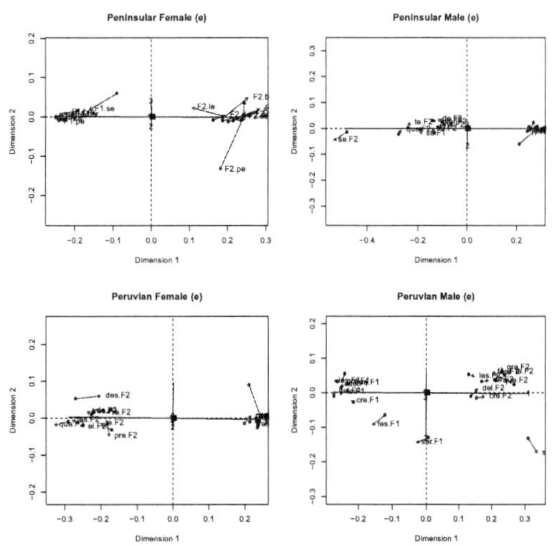

Figure 2: Procrustes plots for /e/ sounds for all groups and genders. Longer arrows display larger displacements between original and enhanced tokens. As seen in the projections, Peruvian vowels tend to be higher.

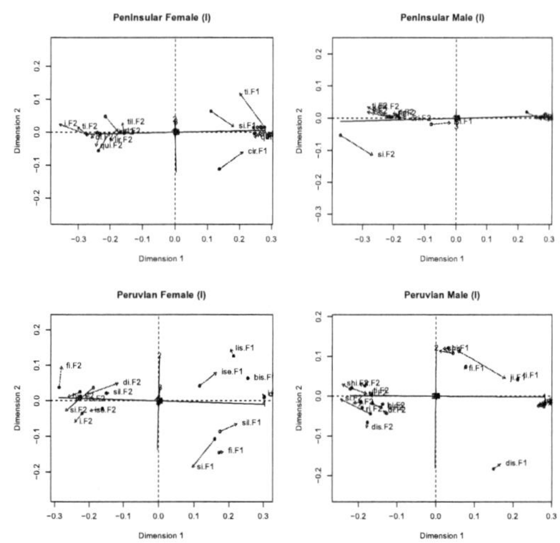

Figure 3: Procrustes plots for /i/ sounds for all groups and genders. Longer arrows display larger displacements between original and enhanced tokens. As seen in the projections, Peruvian vowels tend to be higher.

The analysis confirmed that the SE techniques employed in this study effectively preserve essential acoustic characteristics of /e/ vowel sounds across different Spanish-speaking populations. The high correlations and significant p-values across demographic groups reinforce the reliability of these enhancement methods in linguistic data. The combined results from the Procrustes analysis and the visual representations underscore the effectiveness of SE in retaining the critical acoustic properties and vocalic quality.

/i/ Sound

This section details the outcomes of the Procrustes analysis comparing the principal component analyses of original and enhanced /i/ vocalic sounds (Figure 3).

For Peninsular Spanish speakers, the Procrustes analysis varied between genders. Female speakers showed a $M_{12} = .082$, suggesting a noticeable deviation between the original and enhanced datasets, albeit less significant than for the /e/ sounds. However, the correlation in a symmetric Procrustes rotation was strong (.957), indicating that the speech enhancement preserved much of the vowel space's structural integrity. The significance of these observations was confirmed with a value $p < .01$. Male speakers exhibited $M_{12} = .051$, lower than the previous group, indicating a more faithful preservation of the original vocal characteristics. The high correlation coefficient (.973) further supported the effectiveness of the SE, with results being statistically significant ($p < .01$).

For Peruvian Spanish speakers, the results were similarly instructive. Female speakers recorded $M_{12} = .086$, which was slightly higher than that observed for Peninsular females, indicating a modest shape difference between the original and enhanced versions. The correlation coefficient was .955, reflecting robust maintenance of vowel characteristics despite the enhancements ($p < .01$). Male speakers, on the other hand, showed an even better alignment ($M_{12} = .047$) and a good correlation (.976), highlighting the small impact of the enhancement process in corrupting the acoustic properties of the sound ($p < .01$).

While some deviations were observed, particularly among female speakers, the overall high correlation values indicate that the enhancements largely preserved the essential acoustic characteristics of the /i/ sound. The results and significance were similar to the results for /e/.

5 Conclusion

In this study, we have analyzed the impact of speech enhancement (SE) on the audio properties of fricative and vocalic sounds in Spanish. We use a sociophonetic case study to test whether results are consistent across original and audio-enhanced tokens. We analyzed the results for voicing and duration in intervocalic /s/, comparing paired models fitted on original and enhanced data. We also inspected the impact of condition as an independent variable on voicing and duration.

In the sociophonetic dimension, our analyses show that while demographic factors such as gender and geographic origin influence certain phonetic features like frication duration, they have minimal impact on others such as voicing. Regarding condition, the experimental manipulation of audio enhancement did not significantly alter the outcomes, indicating robustness in preserving phonetic characteristics. We found no evidence suggesting that the enhanced tokens significantly modified or contaminated the statistical results.

Experiments in vocalic quality showed a similar trend. The features captured by the PCA coincide with previous literature on the comparison between Peruvian and Peninsular vowels. We show that SE tokens preserve essential acoustic characteristics of vocalic sounds across different Spanish-speaking populations. The high correlations and significant outputs across all demographic groups reinforce the reliability of the results.

These findings hold the potential to yield advantageous results for languages with limited resources, which usually have lower-quality speech corpora. By demonstrating the robust preservation of acoustic properties and sociophonetic markers, this study supports the effectiveness of speech enhancement for data in which linguistic nuances are critical.

6 Limitations and Future Work

While informative and representative, this study was limited to a relatively small sample size. Future studies may benefit from examining tokens with different amounts of background noise or more realistic artifacts (e.g., inserting noises at intervals, overlaying background conversations, or low-quality recording equipment simulations). We acknowledge that some field work recordings include background conversations that may have sociolinguistic value for the main footage. Those recordings are out of the reach of this study; however, future work may explore how audio separation models may help isolate primary and background sounds. We provide the perturbation functions and hyperparameter configurations for future scholars to investigate feature fidelity thresholds. Similar study cases may reinforce the results obtained in this work and lead to new linguistically grounded methodologies for audio model benchmarking.

7 Ethics Statement

Aligning with ethical and moral standards, we offer a new method to improve the quality of under-researched language corpora. We acknowledge the intricate nature of linguistic variability and its implications on the societal effects of technology. It is crucial for scholars to contribute to the creation of inclusive systems that accurately represent all members of society. The dissemination of these findings paves the way for a transparent and inclusive dialogue within the academic community that upholds respect for linguistic and cultural diversity. In the same way, we also aim to facilitate the progress of multilingual computational tools.

References

Virginia Best, Simon Carlile, Craig Jin, and André van Schaik. 2005. The role of high frequencies in speech localization. *The Journal of the Acoustical Society of America*, 118(1):353–363.

Michael K Brame and Ivonne Bordelois. 1973. Vocalic alternations in spanish. *Linguistic Inquiry*, 4(2):111–168.

Adelbert W Bronkhorst. 2000. The cocktail party phenomenon: A review of research on speech intelligibility in multiple-talker conditions. *Acta acustica united with acustica*, 86(1):117–128.

Jeremy Calder, Rebecca Wheeler, Sarah Adams, Daniel Amarelo, Katherine Arnold-Murray, Justin Bai, Meredith Church, Josh Daniels, Sarah Gomez, Jacob Henry, et al. 2022. Is zoom viable for sociophonetic research? a comparison of in-person and online recordings for vocalic analysis. *Linguistics Vanguard*, page 20200148.

Kuan Chen, Bo Chen, Jiahao Lai, and Kai Yu. 2018. High-quality voice conversion using spectrogram-based wavenet vocoder. In *Interspeech*, pages 1993–1997.

E Colin Cherry. 1953. Some experiments on the recognition of speech, with one and with two ears. *The Journal of the acoustical society of America*, 25(5):975–979.

Kateřina Chládková, Paola Escudero, and Paul Boersma. 2011. Context-specific acoustic differences between peruvian and iberian spanish vowels. *The Journal of the Acoustical Society of America*, 130(1):416–428.

John R Deller Jr, John G Proakis, and John H Hansen. 1993. *Discrete time processing of speech signals*. Prentice Hall PTR.

Carlos Fonseca. 2023. 120h spanish speech.

Michael S Gradoville, Earl Kjar Brown, and Richard J File-Muriel. 2022. The phonetics of sociophonetics: Validating acoustic approaches to spanish/s. *Journal of Phonetics*, 91:101125.

Adriana Guevara-Rukoz, Isin Demirsahin, Fei He, Shan-Hui Cathy Chu, Supheakmungkol Sarin, Knot Pipatsrisawat, Alexander Gutkin, Alena Butryna, and Oddur Kjartansson. 2020. Crowdsourcing latin american spanish for low-resource text-to-speech. In *Proceedings of The 12th Language Resources and Evaluation Conference (LREC)*, pages 6504–6513, Marseille, France. European Language Resources Association (ELRA).

Umut Isik, Ritwik Giri, Neerad Phansalkar, Jean-Marc Valin, Karim Helwani, and Arvindh Krishnaswamy. 2020. Poconet: Better speech enhancement with frequency-positional embeddings, semi-supervised conversational data, and biased loss.

Ewa Jacewicz, Joshua M Alexander, and Robert A Fox. 2023. Introduction to the special issue on perception and production of sounds in the high-frequency range of human speech. *The Journal of the Acoustical Society of America*, 154(5):3168–3172.

Allard Jongman, Ratree Wayland, and Serena Wong. 2000. Acoustic characteristics of english fricatives. *The Journal of the Acoustical Society of America*, 108(3):1252–1263.

Viktor Kharlamov, Daniel Brenner, and Benjamin V Tucker. 2023. Examining the effect of high-frequency information on the classification of conversationally produced english fricatives. *The Journal of the Acoustical Society of America*, 154(3):1896–1902.

Haohe Liu, Qiuqiang Kong, Qiao Tian, Yan Zhao, DeLiang Wang, Chuanzeng Huang, and Yuxuan Wang. 2021. Voicefixer: Toward general speech restoration with neural vocoder. *Preprint*, arXiv:2109.13731.

Daniel McFadden. 1972. Conditional logit analysis of qualitative choice behavior. *Frontiers in Econometrics, Academic Press*, pages 105–142.

Daniel Michelsanti, Zheng-Hua Tan, Shi-Xiong Zhang, Yong Xu, Meng Yu, Dong Yu, and Jesper Jensen. 2021. An overview of deep-learning-based audio-visual speech enhancement and separation. *IEEE/ACM Transactions on Audio, Speech, and Language Processing*, 29:1368–1396.

Geoffrey Stewart Morrison, Paola Escudero, et al. 2007. A cross-dialect comparison of peninsular-and peruvian-spanish vowels. In *Proceedings of the 16th international Congress of phonetic sciences*, pages 1505–1508. Citeseer.

Tamara Rathcke, Jane Stuart-Smith, Bernard Torsney, and Jonathan Harrington. 2017. The beauty in a beast: Minimising the effects of diverse recording quality on vowel formant measurements in sociophonetic real-time studies. *Speech Communication*, 86:24–41.

Barbara G Shinn-Cunningham and Virginia Best. 2008. Selective attention in normal and impaired hearing. *Trends in amplification*, 12(4):283–299.

Erik R Thomas. 2002. Sociophonetic applications of speech perception experiments. *American speech*, 77(2):115–147.

Erik R Thomas. 2013. Phonetic analysis in sociolinguistics. *Research methods in sociolinguistics: A practical guide*, pages 119–135.

Tomáš Vampola, Jaromír Horáček, Vojtěch Radolf, Jan G Švec, and Anne-Maria Laukkanen. 2020. Influence of nasal cavities on voice quality: Computer simulations and experiments. *The Journal of the Acoustical Society of America*, 148(5):3218–3231.

Aaron Van Den Oord, Sander Dieleman, Heiga Zen, Karen Simonyan, Oriol Vinyals, Alex Graves, Nal Kalchbrenner, Andrew Senior, Koray Kavukcuoglu, et al. 2016. Wavenet: A generative model for raw audio. *arXiv preprint arXiv:1609.03499*, 12.

Chengzhu Yu, Kamil K Wójcicki, Philipos C Loizou, John HL Hansen, and Michael T Johnson. 2014. Evaluation of the importance of time-frequency contributions to speech intelligibility in noise. *The Journal of the Acoustical Society of America*, 135(5):3007–3016.

A Noise Generation

As mentioned in section 3, we modify the samples using Additive White Gaussian Noise (AWGN) implemented through a Python function. The AWGN implemented in this work is defined by

$$RMS = \sqrt{\frac{1}{N}\sum_{i=1}^{N} x_i^2} \quad (1)$$

where we calculate the root mean square (RMS) of a given signal x_i.

We then use Equation 2 to generate random Gaussian noise z_{noise}. We add parameter λ, which is a scaling factor that allows to blend the noise in the background. For the purposes of this study, we used $\lambda = .1$, but other studies may benefit from experimenting with different parameter settings.

$$z_{\text{noise}} = \mathcal{N}(0, (RMS \cdot \lambda)^2) \quad (2)$$

Finally, we combine the original signal x_i with the Gaussian noise z_{noise} to get the corrupted file $x_i{}'$.

$$x_i{}' = x_i + z_{\text{noise}} \quad (3)$$

B Voicing Data

Original Voicing Measurements															
Peninsular Females				Peninsular Males				Peruvian Females				Peruvian Male			
t (s)	*un (s)*	*v (s)*	*v (%)*	*t (s)*	*un (s)*	*v (s)*	*v (%)*	*t (s)*	*un (s)*	*v (s)*	*v (%)*	*t (s)*	*un (s)*	*v (s)*	*v (%)*
.09	.09	0	0	.08	.08	0	0	.13	.11	.02	15.38	.14	.13	.01	7.14
.13	.12	.01	7.69	.09	.08	.01	11.11	.12	.12	0	0	.14	.14	0	0
.1	.09	.01	10.00	.08	.07	.01	12.50	.1	.1	0	0	.13	.12	.01	7.69
.1	.09	.01	10.00	.06	.06	0	0	.1	.09	.01	10.00	.11	.1	.01	9.09
.13	.11	.02	15.38	.06	.06	0	0	.11	.1	.01	9.09	.12	.11	.01	8.33
.12	.11	.01	8.33	.08	.07	.01	12.50	.09	.08	.01	11.11	.13	.13	0	0
.08	.08	0	0	.09	.07	.02	22.22	.09	.09	0	0	.1	.09	.01	10.00
.107	.099	.009	**7.344**	.077	.070	.007	**8.333**	.106	.099	.007	**6.512**	.124	.117	.007	**6.037**

Table 4: Voicing measurement for original tokens with intervocalic fricative (s) across all speakers. The last row indicates mean values.

Enhanced Voicing Measurements															
Peninsular Females				Peninsular Males				Peruvian Females				Peruvian Males			
t (s)	*un (s)*	*v (s)*	*v (%)*	*t (s)*	*un (s)*	*v (s)*	*v (%)*	*t (s)*	*un (s)*	*v (s)*	*v (%)*	*t (s)*	*un (s)*	*v (s)*	*v (%)*
.1	.1	0	0	.08	.08	0	0	.14	.12	.02	14.29	.14	.14	0	0
.13	.13	0	0	.09	.08	.01	11.11	.11	.11	0	0	.14	.13	.01	7.14
.1	.09	.01	10.00	.08	.07	.01	12.50	.11	.1	.01	9.09	.13	.12	.01	7.69
.11	.09	.02	18.18	.08	.07	.01	12.50	.1	.1	0	0	.11	.11	0	0
.13	.12	.01	7.69	.07	.07	0	0	.11	.1	.01	9.09	.11	.1	.01	9.09
.11	.11	0	0	.08	.07	.01	12.50	.09	.08	.01	11.11	.14	.13	.01	7.14
.08	.07	.01	12.50	.08	.07	.01	12.50	.09	.09	0	0	.09	.09	0	0
.109	.101	.007	**6.911**	.080	.073	.007	**8.730**	.107	.100	.007	**6.226**	.123	.117	.006	**4.438**

Table 5: Voicing measurement for enhanced tokens with intervocalic fricative (s) across all speakers. The last row indicates mean values.

C Models

Model	Coefficient	Df	Sum Sq	Mean Sq	F-value	p-value	Df	Sum Sq	Mean Sq	F-value	p-value
Voicing	Country	1	17.1	17.13	.433	.516	1	43.4	43.35	1.236	.277
	Gender	1	.5	.46	.012	.915	1	.0	.00	.000	.994
	Residuals	25	987.9	39.52			25	876.9	35.07		
Duration	Country	1	.003	.003	9	**<.01**	1	.003	.003	7.819	**<.01**
	Gender	1	0	0	.563	.46	1	0	0	.753	.393
	Residuals	25	.01	0			25	.009	0		

Table 6: Results of the ANOVAs for duration and voicing in original (left) and enhanced tokens (right).

Model	Coefficient	Value	Std.Error	t-value	p-value	Value	Std.Error	t-value	p-value
Voicing	Intercept	5.162	2.014	**2.562**	**.016**	4.158	2.009	**2.069**	**.048**
	countrySpain	1.227	2.326	.527	.602	2.46	2.32	1.060	.299
	genderM	-.079	2.326	-.034	.973	.044	2.32	.019	.984
Duration	Intercept	-4.585	.009	**-497.981**	**<.01**	-4.584	.008	**-541.376**	**<.01**
	countrySpain	-.024	.010	-2.2678	.032	-.021	.009	-2.206	.036
	genderM	-.003	.010	-.3655	.717	-.005	.009	-.578	.568

Table 7: Results of the RLMs for duration and voicing in original (left) and enhanced tokens (right).

Random effects	Name	Variance	Std.Dev.		Variance	Std.Dev.		
id	(Intercept)	0	0		0	0		
	Residual	46.48	6.818		45.55	6.749		
Fixed effects	Estimate	Std. Error	t value	p value	Estimate	Std. Error	t value	p value
(Intercept)	5.169	2.288	**2.259**	**.032**	4.085	2.265	1.803	.083
countrySpain	1.176	2.643	.445	.660	2.4005	2.616	.917	.367
genderM	-.130	2.643	-.05	.960	.1474	2.616	.056	.955

Table 8: Results of the RLMEMs for voicing in original (left) and enhanced tokens (right).

Random Effects	Name	Variance	Std.Dev.	Name	Variance	Std.Dev.		
id	(Intercept)	0	.027	(Intercept)	0	.027		
	Residual	0	.017	Residual	0	.015		
Fixed effects	Estimate	Std. Error	t value	p value	Estimate	Std. Error	t value	p value
(Intercept)	-4.584	.024	**-185.33**	**<.01**	-4.585	.024	**-185.56**	**<.01**
countrySpain	-.022	.028	-.79	.436	-.020	.028	-.71	.484
genderM	-.005	.028	-.2	.843	-.005	.028	-.18	.858

Table 9: Results of the RLMEMs for duration in original (left) and enhanced tokens (right).

Comparing Kaldi-Based Pipeline Elpis and Whisper for Čakavian Transcription

Austin Jones[1*], Shulin Zhang[1*], John Hale[1],
Margaret E. L. Renwick[1], Zvjezdana Vrzić[2], Keith Langston[1]
[1]Department of Linguistics, University of Georgia, Athens GA USA
[2]Department of Linguistics, New York University, New York NY USA
austin.jones25@uga.edu shulin.zhang@uga.edu jthale@uga.edu
mrenwick@uga.edu zvjezdana.vrzic@nyu.edu langston@uga.edu

Abstract

Automatic speech recognition (ASR) has the potential to accelerate the documentation of endangered languages, but the dearth of resources poses a major obstacle. Čakavian, an endangered variety spoken primarily in Croatia, is a case in point, lacking transcription tools that could aid documentation efforts. We compare training a new ASR model on a limited dataset using the Kaldi-based ASR pipeline Elpis to using the same dataset to adapt the transformer-based pretrained multilingual model Whisper, to determine which is more practical in the documentation context. Results show that Whisper outperformed Elpis, achieving the lowest average Word Error Rate (WER) of 57.3% and median WER of 35.48%. While Elpis offers a less computationally expensive model and friendlier user experience, Whisper appears better at adapting to our collected Čakavian data.

1 Introduction

The low-resource nature of language documentation challenges the capabilities of current ASR tools due to a lack of pretrained language models (Johnson et al., 2018). This challenge becomes greater when the linguistic context exhibits a high degree of variation, including code-switching. Čakavian, an endangered (EGIDS 6b) language with approximately 50,000 total speakers (Eberhard et al., 2024), represents one such situation. While traditionally considered a dialect of Croatian, it differs substantially from standard Croatian and colloquial Štokavian varieties spoken by the majority of the Croatian population.[1] In addition to differences in phonology, morphology, and syntax, the Čakavian lexicon includes many borrowings from Romance as well as a number of forms of Slavic origin that are not typical for other Croatian varieties (Langston, 2020; Vuković and Langston, 2020). See Table 7 and Table 8 for some examples. Although Čakavian is not severely endangered, individual local varieties in this region may vary significantly from one another and have few speakers. Prior research exploring the capabilities of currently available ASR systems to this context find that (standard) Croatian transcription models struggle with the differences present between the two languages (Zhang et al., 2024). Therefore, further experimentation can provide insight into best practices for documentation efforts. As part of a larger project (ELIC) to create a spoken corpus documenting endangered language varieties in Istria-Kvarner, Croatia (Langston et al., 2023), this study compares the performance of the Kaldi-based transcription pipeline Elpis (Foley et al., 2018) and the transformer-based multilingual ASR model Whisper (Radford et al., 2023) on the transcription of Čakavian interview data.

Elpis offers a locally executable pipeline to train new ASR models using Kaldi (Povey et al., 2011). GMM-based systems like Elpis are less computationally demanding and they require relatively less training data compared to neural networks. This is crucial for language documentation because pretrained tools rarely exist. Given that field linguists often lack the necessary expertise and access to high-powered computational resources, complexity is an important factor. Conversely, the demands of large multilingual ASR models could prove justifiable if they can generalize to new contexts. (Radford et al., 2023). The transformer-based multilingual ASR model Whisper can be adapted with user data from any language. The base model includes at least 91 hours of unspecified Croatian data, which almost certainly does not include Čakavian speech, due to the lack of available resources. While we argue that Čakavian is distinct from Croa-

*These authors contributed equally to this work and share first authorship.

[1]The traditional names for these varieties, Čakavian and Štokavian, are based on the different words for 'what', *ča* and *što*.

Proceedings of the 3rd Workshop on NLP Applications to Field Linguistics (Field Matters 2024), pages 61–68
August 16, 2024 ©2024 Association for Computational Linguistics

tian[2], the availability of a related model means linguists need not train a neural network from scratch. We utilize Whisper large-v3. (Radford et al., 2023). Our results find that the best performing fine-tuned Whisper model [3] is able to outperform Elpis on a sample of 3 Čakavian interviews, achieving an average WER of 57.3% and median WER of 35.48%, while Elpis achieved an average WER of 130.1% and median WER of 129%.

2 Data and Methods

To compare model creation using Elpis and model adaptation using Whisper, 5.7 hours of audio data were used for training. This included five interviews of different native speakers of Čakavian and one audiobook of a Čakavian translation of *The Little Prince* (Saint-Exupéry, 2021; Ljubešić et al., 2024). Table 1 provides a breakdown of the data. Utterance level transcriptions were made by native speakers and linguists with expertise in Čakavian. Both models were trained using the same data. Elpis uses a fixed 90%-10% split for training and testing. For adapting Whisper, an 80%-20% split was used. The resulting models were then evaluated on three additional interviews. Output was compared to manual transcriptions to determine the median WERs discussed in Section 2.3.

Usage	Audio ID	Dialect type	Length (min)	Speaker	Interviewer
Training	ckm001	Istrian ekavian	25	F	M
	ckm002	Coastal ekavian	73	F	F
	ckm004	i/ekavian	30	F	F
	ckm005	i/ekavian	57	F	F
	ckm006	Coastal ekavian	67	F	F
	Audiobook	ikavian	90	M & F	n/a
Testing	ckm009	Istrian ekavian	36	F	M
	ckm015	ikavian	55	F	F
	ckm016	ikavian	119	M	F

Table 1: Speaker information for the Čakavian datasets.

2.1 Elpis Data Preparation

The data are preprocessed according to the Elpis documentation (Foley et al., 2022). The input 16-bit mono WAV files were resampled to 16 kHz. Each audio file had a corresponding ELAN file, in which the speech was transcribed in segments approximately 10 seconds in length. All transcriptions were standardized by removing punctuation, variable spellings, and any other non-lexical information. Further, as advised by the documentation, sections in the transcriptions in which 10% or more of the interviewer's and interviewee's speech overlapped were removed. These sections were not deleted from the audio files. In addition to the WAV audio and ELAN transcription files, the input included a text file containing the grapheme to phoneme rules of Čakavian. Mel Frequency Cepstral Coefficient (MFCC) based feature extraction is performed on the WAV files to derive input sequences. MFCCs reduce acoustic data to focus on frequencies relevant for human perception, capturing relevant information from the input in a compact way. Elpis can perform file conversion, resampling, and transcription standardization during setup; however, we found doing these steps prior to training produced the best results. Users are also able to select the n-gram value (ranging from unigram to 5-gram) during model creation. For our data set (total 3693 words), trigrams gave the best results. The results of models with different n-gram values are not reported here for concision. Lastly, due to the explicit guidance for segmentation length given in the Elpis documentation, we did not test different segmentation windows, as was done for Whisper.

2.2 Whisper Data Preparation

Unlike ELPIS, which was trained entirely on our Čakavian data, Whisper large-v3 (available as "*openai/whisper-large-v3*" (Radford et al., 2023)), is a pre-trained model, which was adapted using our dataset. This pretrained model is an expansion of Whisper large-v2, which was built on approximately 1 million hours of weakly labeled multilingual audio including 91 hours of Croatian data. To create Whisper large-v3, 4 million hours of pseudo-labeled audio collected using Whisper large-v2 was added to the original dataset. To perform adaptation, the training data was prepared as follows. 16-bit mono WAV files were resampled to 16kHz. Transcription segmentation was set according to Whisper documentation to be no longer than 30 seconds. Transcriptions were normalized by standardizing spelling and stripping punctuation and non-lexical items. Segmentation windows of 10 seconds and 20 seconds were also tested. Whisper utilizes log-Mel spectrograms to derive input feature vectors. While these are not as lightweight as MFCCs, they are richer by preserving time course information. This allows them to be more easily interpretable than MFCCs. Lastly, noise based on a random Gaussian distribution was added to each

[2]This is indicated by the poor performance of the base Whisper-v3 model, presumably trained on standard Croatian, in the transcription of Čakavian as shown in Table 2.

[3]The nine fine-tuned Whisper models, as described in Table 2, are available at https://huggingface.co/ninninz as "whisper-ckm-{1-9}".

input file to increase the robustness of the adapted model. Training was performed on an Nvidia A100 GPU with a learning rate of 1e-5. A warm-up step value of 500 was used with a max step of 4000. See Table 2 for details on each model's training data. The median WER was used to guide model selection for evaluation.

2.3 Model Evaluation

During model training, Word Error Rate (WER) values were provided by each system. However, to obtain a more detailed analysis of WER and the types of errors made by each model, a separate evaluation using three different test interviews was performed. The models' output transcription and the manual transcriptions were cleaned to remove punctuation, and all words were converted to lowercase. Second, the manual and model text sequences were force-aligned with the Python module Bio.pairwise2 (Cock et al., 2009). It should be noted that this package made the alignment happen with *perfect* string matches. Therefore, to reduce the penalty for nearly correct transcriptions, a "fuzzy" match was done to allow for the partially correct cases to be considered as *Substitution* cases. The fuzzy match was realized by getting the unmatched sequences between manual and model transcriptions and then calculating pair-words' similarity ratio based on Levenshtein Distance (Yujian and Bo, 2007). For example, as shown in Table 3, the "Manual" column is the original transcription, the "Model" column is the model transcription, and the "Model fuzzy" column shows the realigned results that have achieved a minimum score of 60.

Manual	Model	Model fuzzy	Score	Type
dobro	dobro	dobro	100	c
onda	onda	onda	100	c
moremo		moramo	83	s
	moramo		0	
započet	započet	započet	100	c
s	s	s	100	c
obziron		obzirom	86	s
	obzirom		0	

Table 3: Example of text alignment. See the detailed alignment process in Section 2.3.

After these steps, the text alignment between the model output and manual transcription wasa compared to calculate substitution, insertion, or deletion errors shown in Equation 1. *S* is a count of *Substitution* errors; *D* refers to *Deletion*; *I* refers to *Insertion* and *C* refers to correctly matched cases.

$$WER = \frac{S + D + I}{S + D + C} \tag{1}$$

The matching type, as shown in the "type" column in Table 3, was obtained from string comparison between the "manual" and "model_fuzzy". A correctly matched case is indicated by *c*, while *s* corresponds to a *Substitution* case.

3 Results

As shown in Figure 1, the WER distributions of Elpis, each fine-tuned Whisper model, and the base Whisper model are shown. For all models, "whisper-ckm-3" achieved the lowest average WER of 57.3% and a median WER of 35.48% in the forced-aligned WER evaluation. The median in this context refers to the error for each 20-second transcription segment obtained in the transcription of the test interviews during evaluation. The average WER for all test interview data combined was 57.3%.

3.1 Elpis Pipeline Performance

The best performance by Elpis achieved an average WER of 130.1% on the test data and a median value of 129%. The WER exceeds 100% because the model made many insertion errors. Insertion rates inflated the output transcriptions to include more words than were present in the manual transcription. This model included both the interview and audiobook data. Conversely to Whisper, the audiobook data improved the model's performance. We found that while Elpis required less computational expertise to use, it is more sensitive to the quality of the input data.[4]

3.2 Whisper Model performance

The best performing model of Whisper was adapted using only the interview speech data. The audiobook data was not included. Additionally, a 20-second input transcription segmentation was used, and white noise data augmentation was performed. Model testing showed that the performance is sensitive to training data window size, and white-noise data augmentation improved performance. This is possibly due to the interview data containing noise from the recording environment. Asymmetries in

[4] In testing, the lowest WER reported by Elpis itself was a model trained on the audiobook data alone. We believe this is due to the studio quality of the recordings and lack of speaker overlap. While not used in this paper due to lack of comparability to our Whisper models, it highlights that GMM-based technologies are very input sensitive.

Model	Data	Transcription Segmentation (Seconds)	White Noise	Median WER (%)
whisper-large-v3	Base model	10	N	56.00
whisper-ckm-1	Interview speech	10	N	50.00
whisper-ckm-2	Interview speech	20	N	50.00
whisper-ckm-3	Interview speech	20	Y	35.48
whisper-ckm-4	Interview speech and audiobook	10	Y	53.13
whisper-ckm-5	Interview speech and audiobook	20	Y	83.33
whisper-ckm-6	Interview speech and audiobook	30	Y	58.82
whisper-ckm-7	Interview speech (Speaker overlap removed) and audiobook	10	Y	40.74
whisper-ckm-8	Interview speech (Speaker overlap removed) and audiobook	20	Y	40.91
whisper-ckm-9	Interview speech (Speaker overlap removed) and audiobook	30	Y	55.17

Table 2: All models based on and including whisper-large-v3. Whisper-ckm-{1/2/3} were adapted on Čakavian interview speech data. Whisper-ckm-{4/5/6/7/8/9} were adapted on both the interview speech data and Čakavian audiobook data. "Y" in the white noise column means the input data was augmented with random noise. Median WER is the median error calculated on the three test interviews. (See Section 2.3 for details).

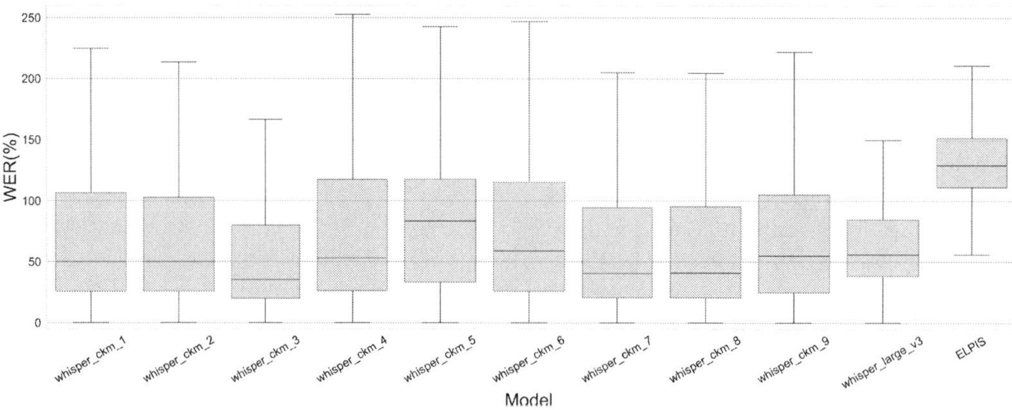

Figure 1: WER value distribution for each model. Value distributions come from the calculated error for each transcription segment across each model and the base whisper model. Values in Appendix Table 5.

the reporting of the input data augmentation in Table 4 are for the sake of brevity. The omissions represent models with higher median WERs.

3.3 Error Type Analysis

As shown in Table 4, a comparison of the models' error type occurrence was carried out. Compared to the base Whisper model ("whisper-large-v3"), the best adapted model ("whisper-ckm-3") achieved a 7.5% WER reduction. This model showed a higher Correct rate and lower Substitution and Deletion rates. Comparatively, Elpis had higher Deletion and Insertion rates, which led to its high WER.

4 Discussion

Our results show that the best-performing model was obtained by adapting Whisper-large-v3 using transcribed interview data. It achieved an average WER of 57.3% and a median WER of 35.48%. Overall, this level of performance is still poor, but the automated transcriptions contain many segments that are largely or completely error-free. We have found in practice that some transcribers can use them successfully as guides to accelerate manual transcription. Further, adapted Whisper models can be shared freely online allowing other researchers to benefit from these documentation efforts. The ability to save and reuse a trained model with Elpis is not transparent and represents a current drawback for the pipeline. Although the WER for our Čakavian ASR model created with Elpis was higher than previously reported WER on other languages (Foley et al., 2018), the system has the advantages of not requiring a pre-trained language model and the underlying technology demands fewer computational resources for im-

Model	Correct (C)	Deletion (D)	Insertion (I)	Substitution (S)	Mean WER
whisper-ckm-3	58.2%	24.0%	22.9%	17.8%	57.3%
Elpis	24.4%	61.4%	54.4%	14.2%	130.1%

Table 4: Model error showing each error type and the total each contributed to the mean WER. The error type rate shown here is accumulated across the three test interviews from Table 1 (*i.e.*, ckm009, ckm015, and ckm016 were transcribed to produce the error rates; see the detailed error type information for each test audio file in Appendix Table 6). The error rate is calculated as "Error Case Number divided by the total word number (*i.e.*, C + S + D)".

plementation. Nevertheless, the scale of the pre-trained base Whisper model and the inclusion of related language data appear to have allowed the model to overcome the variation present in our sample of Čakavian.

Our attempts at fine-tuning the Whisper large-v3 model show the effect of several factors on model performance, including: (1) audio segmentation window size, (2) the type and quality of audio data, and (3) speaker overlaps. Here, the best results were obtained with a model that was trained exclusively on the same type of data as the test audio files (sociolinguistic interviews). The addition of higher quality training data from the audiobook recording did not improve the model performance on the specific test data in this study.

5 Limitations and future research

Not only does the language context pose a challenge itself, but the type of training data used in this study further tests the performance of both Whisper and Elpis. Our data consists of field recordings of sociolinguistic interviews. This introduces both environmental noise and speaker overlap into the data. Other work using Whisper on higher resource languages has shown better performance (Amorese et al., 2023; Graham and Roll, 2024). Crucially, in these studies, the test data was restricted in domain to elicited speech or short readings. Concerning Elpis, data sets containing multiple speakers in one training file are not recommended (Foley et al., 2022). We were also unable to account for the effects of code-switching in our data, which is likely to have impacted performance. Annotating the data to identify specific segments that include code-switching would be time-consuming, especially for closely related varieties such as the ones here. Research into utilizing Whisper on code-switching between French and Kréyòl Gwadloupéyen shows similar results to those reported in this paper (Le Ferrand and Prud'Hommeaux, 2024). Nevertheless, the realities of language documentation mean that data collection cannot always proceed in a way that facilitates ASR model training. More work is needed to better understand how different ASR systems such as Whisper and Elpis respond to less than ideal training data.

Also left for future work is a formal comparison of the time required for an ASR-aided workflow vs. manual transcription of our data. Other researchers have reported similar times for manual transcription vs. correcting an ASR transcription (Gorisch and Schmidt, 2024). Another study concludes that ASR output can be useful for transcription only if the WER is less than 30%, which is considerably lower than the mean WERs reported here (Gaur et al., 2016).

6 Conclusion

Čakavian represents a low-resource context that challenges conventional ASR. There exist no pre-trained models for use, local varieties differ substantially from one another, and speakers employ frequent code-switching to standard Croatian. To lessen transcription time, linguists are faced with modeling the data from scratch or reaching for a related language model to adapt. Our results show that model adaptation is the best practice for the automatic transcription of Čakavian. The collection of clean, high quality training data that better conforms to the design specifications for a tool such as Elpis may allow for the creation of models that provide usable automatic transcriptions, based on a small manually transcribed dataset. However, without such training data, systems like Whisper offer better performance.

7 Acknowledgment

This material is based upon work supported by the National Science Foundation under Grant No. BCS 2220425.

References

Terry Amorese, Claudia Greco, Marialucia Cuciniello, Rosa Milo, Olga Sheveleva, and Neil Glackin. 2023. Automatic speech recognition (ASR) with Whisper: Testing performances in different languages. In *Proceedings of the 1st Sustainable, Secure, and Smart Collaboration Workshop in conjunction with CHITALY 2023-Biannual Conference of the Italian SIGCHI Chapter.*

Peter J. A. Cock, Tiago Antao, Jeffrey T. Chang, Brad A. Chapman, Cymon J. Cox, Andrew Dalke, Iddo Friedberg, Thomas Hamelryck, Frank Kauff, Bartek Wilczynski, and Michiel J. L. de Hoon. 2009. Biopython: freely available Python tools for computational molecular biology and bioinformatics. *Bioinformatics*, 25(11):1422.

David M. Eberhard, Gary F. Simons, and Charles D. Fennig. 2024. *Ethnologue: Languages of the world*, 27. edition. SIL International, Dallas, TX.

Ben Foley, Josh Arnold, Rolando Coto-Solano, Gautier Durantin, Timothy Ellison, Daan van Esch, Scott Heath, Frantisek Kratochvíl, Zara Maxwell-Smith, David Nash, Ola Olsson, Mark Richards, Nay San, Hywel Stoakes, Nick Thieberger, and Janet Wiles. 2018. Building speech recognition systems for language documentation: The CoEDL endangered language pipeline and inference system (Elpis). *The 6th Intl. Workshop on Spoken Language Technologies for Under-Resourced Languages*, 29(6):200–204.

Ben Foley, Daan van Esch, and Nay San. 2022. 36 managing transcription data for automatic speech recognition with Elpis. In Andrea L. Berez-Kroeker, Bradley McDonnel, Eve Koller, and Lauren B. Collister, editors, *The Open Handbook of Linguistic Data Management*. The MIT Press.

Yashesh Gaur, Walter S. Lasecki, Florian Metze, and Jeffrey P. Bigham. 2016. The effects of automatic speech recognition quality on human transcription latency. In *Proceedings of the 13th International Web for All Conference*, W4A '16, New York, NY, USA. Association for Computing Machinery.

Jan Gorisch and Thomas Schmidt. 2024. Evaluating workflows for creating orthographic transcripts for oral corpora by transcribing from scratch or correcting ASR-output. In *Proceedings of the 2024 Joint International Conference on Computational Linguistics, Language Resources and Evaluation (LREC-COLING 2024)*, pages 6564–6574, Torino, Italia. ELRA and ICCL.

Calbert Graham and Nathan Roll. 2024. Evaluating OpenAI's Whisper ASR: Performance analysis across diverse accents and speaker traits. *JASA Express Letters*, 4(2).

Lisa M Johnson, Marianna Di Paolo, and Adrian Bell. 2018. Forced alignment for understudied language varieties: Testing Prosodylab-Aligner with Tongan data. *Language Documentation Conservation*, 12:80–123.

Janneke Kalsbeek. 1998. *The Čakavian dialect of Orbanići near Žminj in Istria*. Rodopi, Amsterdam-Atlanta.

Keith Langston. 2020. Čakavian. In Marc L. Greenberg and Lenore A. Grenoble, editors, *Encyclopedia of Slavic Languages and Linguistics Online*. Brill.

Keith Langston, John Hale, Margaret E.L. Renwick, and Zvjezdana Vrzić. 2023. Endangered languages in contact. `https://elic-corpus.uga.edu`.

Éric Le Ferrand and Emily Prud'Hommeaux. 2024. Automatic transcription of grammaticality judgements for language documentation. In *Proceedings of the Seventh Workshop on the Use of Computational Methods in the Study of Endangered Languages*, pages 33–38.

Nikola Ljubešić, Peter Rupnik, and Tea Perinčić. 2024. Mici_Princ.

Iva Lukežić and Sanja Zubčić. 2007. *Grobnički govor XX. stoljeća*. Katedra Čakavskog sabora Grobnišćine, Rijeka.

Cvjetana Miletić. 2019. *Slovnik kastafskega govora*. Udruga Čakavski senjali, Kastav.

Daniel Povey, Arnab Ghoshal, Gilles Boulianne, Lukáš Burget, Ondřej Glembek, Nagendra Goel, Mirko Hannemann, Petr Motlíček, Yanmin Qian, Petr Schwarz, Jan Silovský, Georg Stemmer, and Karel Veselý. 2011. The Kaldi speech recognition toolkit. In *IEEE 2011 workshop on automatic speech recognition and understanding*. IEEE Signal Processing Society.

Alec Radford, Jong Wook Kim, Tao Xu, Greg Brockman, Christine Mcleavey, and Ilya Sutskever. 2023. Robust speech recognition via large-scale weak supervision. In *Proceedings of the 40th International Conference on Machine Learning*, volume 202 of *Proceedings of Machine Learning Research*, pages 28492–28518. PMLR.

Antoine de Saint-Exupéry. 2021. *Mići princ*. Udruga Calculus–Muzej informatike i Muzej djetinjstva. (Original work published 1943). Tea Perinčić, Trans.

Petar Vuković and Keith Langston. 2020. Croatian. In Lenore A. Grenoble, Pia Lane, and Unn Røyneland, editors, *Linguistic Minorities in Europe Online*. Berlin, Boston: De Gruyter Mouton.

Li Yujian and Liu Bo. 2007. A normalized Levenshtein distance metric. *IEEE transactions on pattern analysis and machine intelligence*, 29(6):1091–1095.

Shulin Zhang, John Hale, Margaret Renwick, Zvjezdana Vrzić, and Keith Langston. 2024. An evaluation of Croatian ASR models for čakavian transcription. In *Proceedings of the 2024 Joint International Conference on Computational Linguistics, Language Resources and Evaluation (LREC-COLING 2024)*, pages 1098–1104, Torino, Italia. ELRA and ICCL.

Appendices

A Values of boxplots shown in Figure 1

	whisper-ckm-1	whisper-ckm-2	whisper-ckm-3	whisper-ckm-4	whisper-ckm-5	whisper-ckm-6	whisper-ckm-7	whisper-ckm-8	whisper-ckm-9	whisper-large-v3	Elpis
count	1157	1157	1157	1157	1157	1157	1157	1157	1157	1157	1053
std	201	480	444	270	219	226	150	169	240	234	201
min	0	0	0	0	0	0	0	0	0	0	43
25%	26	26	20	26	33	26	21	21	25	39	111
50%	50	50	35	53	83	59	41	41	55	56	129
75%	107	103	80	118	118	115	95	96	105	85	152
max	3700	10900	8600	7000	6600	4700	3000	3100	3300	3000	2500

Table 5: Descriptive statistics of Models' WER(%) distribution shown in Figure 1

B Detailed error rate for the test audio files

Model	Test Audio	Error Type Case Number				WER
		Correct (C)	*Deletion (D)*	*Insertion (I)*	*Substitution (S)*	
whisper-large-v3	ckm009	3076	838	1125	926	59.7%
	ckm015	4283	2854	2246	1046	75.1%
	ckm016	8001	2645	2687	2728	60.3%
	Total	15360	6337	6058	4700	64.8%
whisper-ckm-3	ckm009	3639	660	1383	588	53.8%
	ckm015	4754	2855	1999	670	66.7%
	ckm016	9945	1690	3603	1802	52.8%
	Total	18338	5205	6985	3060	57.3%
ELPIS	ckm009	1668	2389	2595	838	118.9%
	ckm015	2260	4921	4460	1120	126.5%
	ckm016	1998	7624	6180	1493	137.6%
	Total	5926	14934	13235	3451	130.1%

Table 6: Detailed error rates for the test audio files. The detailed error case numbers for each error type are shown in this table, and the total value is shown in Table 4.

C Examples of characteristic differences between standard Croatian and Čakavian varieties

Standard Croatian	Orbanići	Kastav	Grobnik	Gloss
štȍ	čȁ	čȁ	čȁ	‘what’
tkȍ	kȋ	kȋ	kȋ	‘who’
kòjī	kȋ	kȋ	kȋ	‘which’
gdjȅ	kadȅ	kadȅ	kadȉ, kȃj	‘where’
mlijéko	mliekȍ	mlēkȍ	mlīkȍ	‘milk’
mjȅsēc	mȅsec	mȅsēc	mȉsēc	‘month, moon’
pòsao	dȅlo, pȍsal	dȅlo, posãl	dȅlo, posȃl	‘work, job’
rȅći [rétc̣ì], PRS.1SG rȅčēm	rȅć [ret^{j}], PRS.1SG rečȅn	rȅć [ret^{j}], PRS.1SG rečȅn	rȅć [ret^{j}], PRS.1SG rečȇn	‘say, tell’
rȍđen	rȍjen	rȍjen	rȍjēn, rȍd’ēn	‘born’
pȁs, GEN.SG psȁ	brȅk, GEN.SG brekȁ	pȁs, GEN.SG pasȁ	pȁs, GEN.SG pasȁ	‘dog’
u	v, va	v, va	v, va	‘in’

Table 7: Differences of phonological/morphological origin (incl. some additional lexical differences)(Kalsbeek, 1998; Miletić, 2019; Lukežić and Zubčić, 2007)

Standard Croatian	Orbanići	Kastav	Grobnik	Gloss
dijéte	otrȍk (or dītȅ)	otrȍk	otrȍk (or dītȅ)	‘child’
gládan	lȁčan	lȁčān	lȁčān	‘hungry’
PRS.1SG ȉdēm	griȅn	grȅn	grȇn, rȇn	‘I go’
mȃlī, màlen	mȋći, mȉnji	mīćī	mȋćī	‘small’
odijélo	veštȋt	veštȋd	veštȋd, vestȋd	‘suit’
pȍslije	pȍkle, pȍtle	pȍkle, pȍtle	pȍkli, pȍkla, pȍtla	‘after’
ȕgao	kantuȏn	kāntũn	kāntȗn	‘corner’
ùhvatiti	ćapȁt	ćapȁt	ćapȁt	‘catch, snatch’
zaùstaviti (se), prèstati	frmȁt (se), fermȁt (se)	fērmȁt (se)	fērmȁt (se)	‘stop’

Table 8: Lexical differences (incl. some phonological differences within Čakavian)(Kalsbeek, 1998; Miletić, 2019; Lukežić and Zubčić, 2007)

Zero-shot Cross-lingual POS Tagging for Filipino

Jimson Paulo Layacan, Isaiah Edri W. Flores, Katrina Bernice M. Tan, Ma. Regina E. Estuar, Jann Railey E. Montalan, Marlene M. De Leon
Ateneo Social Computing Lab, Department of Information Systems and Computer Science
Ateneo de Manila University
Quezon City, Philippines

Abstract

Supervised learning approaches in NLP, exemplified by POS tagging, rely heavily on the presence of large amounts of annotated data. However, acquiring such data often requires significant amount of resources and incurs high costs. In this work, we explore zero-shot cross-lingual transfer learning to address data scarcity issues in Filipino POS tagging, particularly focusing on optimizing source language selection. Our zero-shot approach demonstrates superior performance compared to previous studies, with top-performing fine-tuned PLMs achieving F1 scores as high as 79.10%. The analysis reveals moderate correlations between cross-lingual transfer performance and specific linguistic distances–featural, inventory, and syntactic–suggesting that source languages with these features closer to Filipino provide better results. We identify tokenizer optimization as a key challenge, as PLM tokenization sometimes fails to align with meaningful representations, thus hindering POS tagging performance.

1 Introduction

The rise of pretrained language models (PLMs) has revolutionized the landscape of natural language processing (NLP). While these models demonstrably address data scarcity in under-resource languages by learning universal language representations (Qiu et al., 2020), many languages, including Filipino, a widely spoken under-resource language in the Philippines (Lewis, 2009), continue to face significant challenges. Building robust NLP pipelines for Filipino remains difficult despite the abundance of textual resources like literary works, linguistic references, and social media data.

Filipino lacks dedicated resources for a range of language processing tasks (Aquino and de Leon, 2020; Cruz and Cheng, 2021; Miranda, 2023). Robust and reliable part-of-speech (POS) taggers could significantly improve the performance of such tasks by accurately classifying words into their grammatical categories. This disambiguation is essential because many words can have multiple meanings based on context. For example, the Filipino word "buhay" can be a "pangngalan" (noun) meaning "life" or a "pang-uri" (adjective) meaning "lively" or "vibrant." By clearing up word confusion, POS tagging helps in performing higher-level NLP tasks such as machine translation, information extraction, text-to-speech conversion, speech recognition, etc.

However, annotating datasets for POS tagging is complex and resource-intensive. One potential solution is cross-lingual transfer learning, which involves using the knowledge gained from training a model in one language to address tasks in another language (Kim et al., 2017). In this paradigm, a language model acquires representations from a source language and then undergoes fine-tuning to execute tasks in a target language with limited labeled data. Furthermore, zero-shot learning, a specific form of cross-lingual transfer learning, presents a solution in scenarios with a complete absence of annotated data (de Vries et al., 2022).

One crucial factor in enhancing zero-shot cross-lingual transfer learning is the selection of the source language. This selection process involves identifying and analyzing language similarity metrics that can improve the success of cross-lingual transfer learning (Eronen et al., 2023). These metrics quantify and compare linguistic and structural correspondences between languages.

Linguists often use intuitive notions of structure to compare languages (Stabler and Keenan, 2003), and source language selection tends to follow similar intuitive approaches. However, quantified language similarity metrics provide a more objective basis for these comparisons, suggesting that higher similarity between a source-target language pair generally results in improved cross-lingual transfer learning performance. The challenge, however, lies in selecting the most appropriate similarity metric,

Proceedings of the 3rd Workshop on NLP Applications to Field Linguistics (Field Matters 2024), pages 69–77
August 16, 2024 ©2024 Association for Computational Linguistics

given the wide array of available options. Identifying which metrics are most indicative of successful cross-lingual transfer learning could streamline the source language selection process, thereby enhancing adaptability for under-resource languages such as Filipino.

Prior studies have explored the impact of several linguistic features on cross-lingual transfer performance. One study emphasized the correlation between linguistic similarity and transfer performance, advocating for selecting source languages based on rigorous linguistic assessments rather than defaulting to English (Eronen et al., 2023). In contrast, another study proposed exploring syntactic and morphological similarities across languages to improve model transfer capabilities (Philippy et al., 2023). Additionally, another study emphasized the importance of including linguistically similar languages in pre-training for improved transfer learning outcomes (de Vries et al., 2022). Our paper extends this line of research by examining linguistic similarity distances between Filipino and source languages and within the context of zero-shot learning for POS tagging.

More specifically, we examined how measures of linguistic distances across multiple dimensions contributed to the effectiveness of POS tagging. While a study (Philippy et al., 2023) investigated this aspect for the Natural Language Inference (NLI) task across all 15 languages in the XNLI dataset (Conneau et al., 2018) individually, our focus is on POS tagging and Filipino as the target language. Futhermore, we investigated how the choice of PLM influenced the outcome and effectiveness of source language selection. We also explored which source language and combination of source languages yielded the highest F1 scores for Filipino POS tagging.

2 Language Similarity

Lang2vec (Littell et al., 2017) is a versatile tool for linguistic analysis that provides readily available pre-computed distances between languages represented as vectors of featural, syntactic, geographic, inventory, genetic, and phonological dimensions from multiple databases including the World Atlas of Language Structures (WALS) (Dryer and Haspelmath, 2013), Syntactic Structures of World Languages (SSWL) (Collins and Kayne, 2009), PHOIBLE (Moran and McCloy, 2019), Glottolog (Hammarström et al., 2018) tree of language families, and Ethnologue (Lewis, 2009). These dimensions enable comparisons of various linguistic features across different languages. Understanding cross-lingual transfer performance in Filipino POS tagging will benefit an investigation of language similarity metrics.

- **Featural Distance** is the cosine distance between vectors defined by features across multiple databases. If a feature value is unknown in one of the languages, it is excluded from the calculation.
- **Genetic Distance** is based on the Glottolog tree of language families, calculated as the distance between two languages in the tree.
- **Geographic Distance** is the shortest distance between two languages on the Earth's sphere, also known as orthodromic distance.
- **Syntactic, Phonological, and Inventory distances** are computed based on specific features identified in the databases, distinguishing between syntactic, phonological, and inventory features.

3 Methods

We used a selection of PLMs, including XLM-R (Conneau et al., 2019), a multilingual variant of the RoBERTa model, and RoBERTa-Tagalog (Cruz and Cheng, 2021), a RoBERTa model pretrained using a Filipino-language pretraining corpus. In this study, both models were finetuned and assessed in a zero-shot cross-lingual scenario, tasked with performing POS tagging for Filipino texts using their base configurations. XLM-R was selected for its well-established performance in multilingual contexts and its robustness in handling large-scale text datasets across various sequence-labeling tasks (Qiu et al., 2020). RoBERTa-Tagalog, on the other hand, was chosen because it is an improvement over the previous Tagalog pretrained Transformer models (Cruz and Cheng, 2021).

3.1 PLM Fine-tuning

Two modeling approaches were employed. First, each PLM was finetuned on data from a single source language and then used to predict POS tags for Filipino text without any further training. This approach assesses the models' ability to generalize to a new language based on their knowledge of the source language. Second, the better-performing

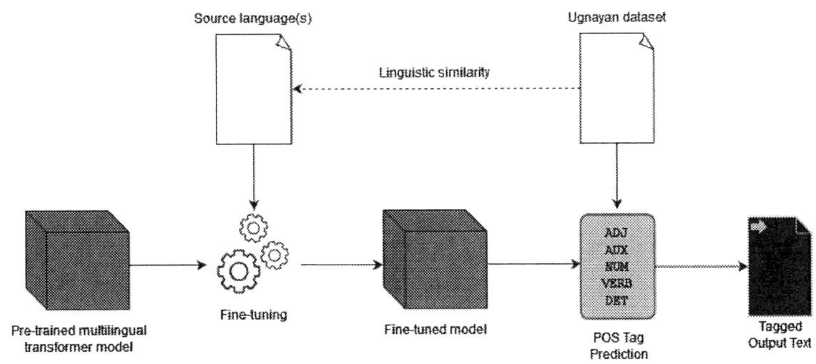

Figure 1: Methodological pipeline for developing POS tagging models (Eronen et al., 2023)

PLM was finetuned on data from several source languages using a progressive approach inspired by curriculum learning (Bengio et al., 2009), adding languages one at a time, starting from the top-performing source language in the monolingual training. This strategy leverages information from related languages, potentially improving the generalizability of the PLM by exposing it to a broader training data.

All models were trained with the same hyperparameter settings. Specifically, the models were trained for 1,000 batches, each containing 10 samples, using a linearly decreasing learning rate starting at 5e-5. These hyperparameters were chosen based on De Vries's configuration (de Vries et al., 2022), which employed a comprehensive transfer learning setup with multiple source and target languages for POS tagging.

3.2 Training and Testing Data

The training dataset for the PLMs was sourced from the Universal Dependencies (UD) 2.13 dataset (De Marneffe et al., 2021). This dataset is designed to facilitate cross-lingual learning and parsing projects by providing a consistent annotation framework across multiple languages. Only languages with available training data were included in this study, with no additional eliminations, as the focus was on establishing a comprehensive setup for a single target language: Filipino.

The UD framework is built on linguistic typology and supports comparisons across languages through consistent annotation. It includes 17 Universal POS (UPOS) tags and comprises 259 treebanks for 148 languages. Below is a list of the UPOS tags used in the dataset (see Table 1).

Table 1: Universal POS (UPOS) Tags

Tag	Description
ADJ	Adjective
ADP	Adposition
ADV	Adverb
AUX	Auxiliary
CCONJ	Coordinating Conjunction
DET	Determiner
INTJ	Interjection
NOUN	Noun
NUM	Numeral
PART	Particle
PRON	Pronoun
PROPN	Proper Noun
PUNCT	Punctuation
SCONJ	Subordinating Conjunction
SYM	Symbol
VERB	Verb
X	Other

Note that the varying quality of UD datasets is a limitation. Some corpora lack diversity in writing styles, and UD updates are inconsistent across languages, with some shifting towards language-specific features and augmented dependencies while fundamental syntactic structures remain problematic (Iwamoto et al., 2021). This may have impacted our cross-lingual transfer learning results, as model performance is sensitive to training data quality.

The finetuned models were evaluated on the Ugnayan dataset (Aquino and de Leon, 2020), which is a standard benchmark for Filipino POS tagging. The performance of these models was measured using the F1 score. This dataset includes 94 sentences with 1011 manually annotated tokens. The Ugnayan dataset, sourced from resources on the Philippines' Department of Education Learning Resource Portal, provides a broad range of sentence structures and syntactic phenomena, utilizing 14 out of the 17 UPOS tags.

3.3 Language Similarity and Learning Performance

The linguistic distances between Filipino and source languages were extracted across various dimensions. These distances were represented as normalized values, creating lists of distances between Filipino and each respective source language. For instance, syntactic distances quantified the similarity between syntax features of Filipino and other languages, with values ranging from 0 to 1.

Each of these lists was then subjected to correlation analysis with the F1 scores obtained from the finetuned models, both XLM-R and RoBERTa-Tagalog. The correlation analysis involved computing Pearson's correlation coefficients to quantify the relationship between language distances and cross-lingual transfer performance. Significance testing was conducted to assess the statistical significance of the observed correlations.

4 Results

The results of the top-performing finetuned PLMs outperform all previously presented zero-shot learning methods listed in Table 2. Specifically, the approach utilizing single-source language fine-tuning achieved the highest F1 score of 79.10%, representing a significant improvement over the highest score achieved by previous methods (Aquino and de Leon, 2022). This improvement demonstrates the effectiveness of the fine-tuning methodology for PLMs, particularly for Filipino POS tagging.

Table 2: Previous zero-shot methods (Aquino and de Leon, 2022) and their corresponding F1 scores for POS tagging on the Ugnayan dataset

Zero-shot Method	F1
UDify (zero-shot baseline)	59.80
POS tag conversion (MGNN)	68.19
POS projection (en)	61.17
POS projection (en+id+it+pl)	61.90

Table 3 shows that, for XLM-R, Afrikaans emerged as the top-performing source language, despite its distant relation to Filipino. Afrikaans is a Germanic language, while Filipino is Austronesian, placing them in very different language families. However, this unexpected result suggests that the two seemingly different languages share some linguistic features.

Table 3: Top 10 best-performing source languages for XLM-R monolingual fine-tuning

Rank	XLM-R	F1
1	Afrikaans	79.10
2	Hebrew	77.02
3	Bulgarian	77.00
4	Vietnamese	76.78
5	Norwegian	75.83
6	Urdu	75.47
7	Czech	75.40
8	Persian	75.36
9	Faroese	75.36
10	English	75.33

Table 4: Top 10 best-performing source languages for RoBERTa-Tagalog monolingual fine-tuning

Rank	RoBERTa-Tagalog	F1
1	English	71.63
2	Naija/Nigerian Pidgin	45.94
3	Serbian	42.47
4	Manx-Cadhan	42.04
5	Slovenian	41.22
6	Spanish	41.20
7	Dutch	41.19
8	Croatian	41.12
9	Polish	40.76
10	Irish	40.35

One potential similarity is their flexible word order, which allows for both subject-verb-object (SVO) and verb-subject-object (VSO) constructions. Additionally, both Afrikaans and Filipino utilize the Latin writing system, albeit with distinct orthographic conventions and phonetic representations. Furthermore, they share the use of affixes to denote verb tense and lack subject-verb agreement (Lewis, 2009; Comrie, 1989). While Afrikaans does exhibit some cognates with Malay, another Austronesian language akin to Filipino, these similarities are still insufficient to claim a structural relationship.

In contrast, Table 4 shows that RoBERTa-Tagalog's top performers are English and Naija. English, as a global lingua franca, shares a rich history with Filipino, likely resulting in lexical borrowings and syntactic influences. Similarly, Naija/Nigerian Pidgin, though distinct, shares linguistic features with English, particularly simplified verb conjugation systems (Lewis, 2009; Comrie, 1989).

Despite these similarities, descriptive observations alone are insufficient to suggest a meaningful structural connection between Filipino and the source languages. The similarities are also not easily generalizable with the other top-performing source languages. Therefore, an examination of quantitative linguistic distances is crucial for optimal source language selection.

4.1 Analysis of Language Similarity Metrics

Correlation analysis was conducted to investigate the relationship between the zero-shot cross-lingual transfer F1 scores of XLM-R and RoBERTa-Tagalog models and various linguistic similarity distances. Pearson's correlation coefficients and their corresponding p-values were calculated to assess the strength and significance of these relationships.

Table 5: Correlation analysis for XLM-R with various linguistic distances

Distances	ρ	**p-value**
Featural	-0.319	0.005
Genetic	-0.089	0.448
Geographic	0.106	0.365
Inventory	-0.236	0.042
Phonological	-0.106	0.368
Syntactic	-0.365	0.001

Table 6: Correlation analysis for RoBERTa-Tagalog with various linguistic distances

Distances	ρ	**p-value**
Featural	-0.233	0.044
Genetic	-0.094	0.421
Geographic	0.304	0.008
Inventory	-0.316	0.006
Phonological	-0.138	0.237
Syntactic	-0.204	0.079

The analysis revealed a relationship between linguistic similarity and the zero-shot cross-lingual transfer performance of both models. Negative correlations, typically between -0.2 and -0.3, were observed with featural, inventory, and syntactic distances. This suggests that as these distances increase, indicating that languages are becoming less similar, the cross-lingual performance of both models tends to decline. These correlations were statistically significant, with p-values below 0.05. Notably, RoBERTa-Tagalog exhibited a weak but statistically significant positive correlation (0.304) with geographic distance, while this correlation for XLM-R was not significant. The genetic and phonological correlations with both models were weaker and not statistically significant.

These findings highlight the importance of considering linguistic similarity when choosing source languages for zero-shot transfer learning. Languages with closer features, inventory, and syntax tend to show better transfer performance for both XLM-R and RoBERTa-Tagalog. Interestingly, RoBERTa-Tagalog seems to benefit, to some extent, from geographic proximity, although higher performance is observed with source languages farther apart from Filipino.

Understanding which linguistic distances significantly correlate with cross-lingual transfer performance is strategic for source language selection. This can be done by prioritizing languages with favorable distances that positively impact transfer learning success.

4.2 Impact of PLM Selection

The experiments highlight the importance of PLM selection in influencing the performance of cross-lingual transfer learning. Since the target language in this study is Filipino, it might be reasonable to expect that RoBERTa-Tagalog would perform competitively. However, the results show that XLM-R outperforms RoBERTa-Tagalog based on F1 scores.

The superior performance of XLM-R may be due to the fact that while RoBERTa-Tagalog is specifically tailored for Tagalog, XLM-R's multilingual pretraining exposed it to a wider range of languages. This diversity of languages enabled XLM-R to recognize a greater variety of linguistic patterns. The architecture of XLM-R may have provided it with a stronger ability to adapt to new languages compared to RoBERTa-Tagalog.

Moreover, there is a notable difference in the top 10 source languages between XLM-R and RoBERTa-Tagalog. This divergence likely reflects how each model adapted distinct linguistic information during fine-tuning, which influenced their performance in transferring knowledge to a new language. Despite RoBERTa-Tagalog's specialization for Tagalog, the specific linguistic characteristics that XLM-R excelled with may not have optimally aligned with Tagalog's features, leading to its lower performance.

4.3 Investigating Multilingual Source Languages

This study also investigated the implementation of a multilingual source language approach for both PLMs. The methodology employed a progressive strategy, beginning with the single best-performing source language and sequentially including additional languages from the top ten performers into the training dataset.

This approach helped us isolate the impact of each additional language on POS tagging performance. Sequentially adding languages can be seen as a blocking strategy akin to curriculum learning (Lee et al., 2023). However, this top-down approach may not always be optimal. Selecting examples and their order can significantly accelerate learning in curriculum learning (Bengio et al., 2009). In this study, we use the monolingual performance of source languages as a measure of how easy it is for the model to "learn" a language.

While the multilingual source language approach did not surpass the highest F1 score achieved by monolingual source training, the results demonstrate promising performance. This setup suggests the potential benefits of simultaneously learning from multiple languages, which allows for the learning of diverse linguistic patterns and structures. Notably, adding more and more languages did not lead to drastic changes in performance. For both XLM-R and RoBERTa-Tagalog, multilingual source training achieved F1 scores in the range of 70% to 80%.

Table 7: F1 scores of XLM-R and RoBERTa-Tagalog with multilingual source languages (top-down approach)

Combination	XLM-R	RoBERTa-Tagalog
1 language	79.10	71.63
2 languages	79.06	71.08
3 languages	76.14	74.49
4 languages	77.55	75.68
5 languages	76.33	73.11

We also tested a random addition of source languages instead of the top-down approach starting from the top source language in terms of performance. We observed that systematically adding sources is slightly better, but the difference is not substantial. At this point, the difference between the two approaches is minimal. Therefore, other approaches can be experimented with in the future.

Table 8: F1 scores of XLM-R and RoBERTa-Tagalog with multilingual source languages (random addition)

Combination	XLM-R	RoBERTa-Tagalog
1 language	79.10	71.63
2 languages	75.58	73.99
3 languages	75.29	71.91
4 languages	77.55	72.97
5 languages	79.01	72.51

4.4 PLM Tokenization

Although zero-shot learning using PLMs has shown promising results for Filipino POS tagging, one main challenge in refining PLMs is optimizing tokenizers. These tokenizers are often inadequate when confronted with previously unseen data variations (Blaschke et al., 2023). This issue is evident when Filipino input texts make model output erroneous parsing, automatically causing incorrect tags.

For instance, upon analyzing the tokenization of the sample input sentence "Tila ang bango ng bulaklak dahil napapikit siya at napangiti." using the RoBERTa-Tagalog model trained on English, an instance of incorrect tokenization was observed. Specifically, the word "napapikit" was split into "napapik" and "it," mistakenly labeled as a verb and adjective, rather than recognizing its actual function as a verb alone.

In another example sentence, "Sa pagpataw ng suspension laban sa Noveras, inamin naman ng Ombudsman na walang matibay na ebidensiya," tokens are incorrectly split and merged. "Sa pagpataw" should be split into "Sa" (adposition) and "pagpataw" (noun), but they have been tokenized as "sa pagp" and "ataw," due to the model's limited exposure to variations in Filipino text. These tokenization errors indicate a lack of sensitivity to the morphological structure of Filipino words. Note that similar problems occur with other source languages and with the XLM-R model.

Despite linguistic similarities from the source languages, Filipino text tokenization using PLMs sometimes fails to align with meaningful representations, leading to poor performance in POS tagging. These errors in tokenization indicate limitations in processing the linguistic nuances of Filipino text.

Another note is that there is variability in the fertility scores across different languages when evaluated. The average tokenizer fertility for each training dataset is reported in Appendix C. This variability suggests the importance of using controlled training data to achieve reliable model performance across languages, as it can significantly affect the performance of the source languages. Future works should consider these variations when selecting and preparing datasets for transfer learning tasks, as they may have an impact on model training and evaluation.

5 Conclusion

This study implements zero-shot fine-tuning using PLMs for Filipino POS tagging, exploring the role of linguistic distances in source language selection. Correlation analysis between linguistic similarity distances and PLM performance suggests that featural, inventory, and syntactic distances between source languages and Filipino, impact cross-lingual transfer learning outcomes.

The study also explored the role of PLM selection in influencing cross-lingual transfer learning performance. While RoBERTa-Tagalog is specifically designed for Tagalog, the multilingual language model XLM-R outperformed it. Furthermore, the exploration of a multilingual source language approach shows good results, though slightly lower than monolingual fine-tuning, suggesting potential benefits of using multiple languages simultaneously for cross-lingual transfer learning tasks.

Despite promising results, challenges in tokenization were observed, particularly in accurately tokenizing Filipino text. Errors in tokenization underscore the need for improved tokenization processes for PLMs, especially for under-resourced languages like Filipino.

Future research should address these challenges by creating new treebanks and expanding existing ones to further enhance model performance. Using top-performing models from this study to annotate unannotated datasets can serve as a foundation for future researches. These annotations, once manually refined, can produce gold-standard annotations for improved training and evaluation of NLP models.

Acknowledgments

We wish to express our sincere gratitude to those who provided support and guidance throughout the development of this paper. We would like to thank the Ateneo Social Computing Lab for providing a supportive academic environment for conducting this research.

References

Angelina Aquino and Franz de Leon. 2020. Parsing in the absence of related languages: Evaluating low-resource dependency parsers on Tagalog. In *Proceedings of the Fourth Workshop on Universal Dependencies (UDW 2020)*, pages 8–15.

Angelina Aquino and Franz de Leon. 2022. Zero-shot and few-shot approaches for tokenization, tagging, and dependency parsing of Tagalog text. In *Proceedings of the 36th Pacific Asia Conference on Language, Information and Computation*, pages 190–202.

Yoshua Bengio, Jérôme Louradour, Ronan Collobert, and Jason Weston. 2009. Curriculum learning. In *Proceedings of the 26th Annual International Conference on Machine Learning*, pages 41–48.

Verena Blaschke, Hinrich Schütze, and Barbara Plank. 2023. Does manipulating tokenization aid cross-lingual transfer? A study on POS tagging for non-standardized languages. *arXiv preprint arXiv:2304.10158*.

Chris Collins and Richard Kayne. 2009. Syntactic structures of the world's languages. *New York: New York University*.

Bernard Comrie. 1989. *Language universals and linguistic typology: Syntax and morphology*. University of Chicago press.

Alexis Conneau, Kartikay Khandelwal, Naman Goyal, Vishrav Chaudhary, Guillaume Wenzek, Francisco Guzmán, Edouard Grave, Myle Ott, Luke Zettlemoyer, and Veselin Stoyanov. 2019. Unsupervised cross-lingual representation learning at scale. *arXiv preprint arXiv:1911.02116*.

Alexis Conneau, Guillaume Lample, Ruty Rinott, Adina Williams, Samuel R Bowman, Holger Schwenk, and Veselin Stoyanov. 2018. XNLI: Evaluating cross-lingual sentence representations. *arXiv preprint arXiv:1809.05053*.

Jan Christian Blaise Cruz and Charibeth Cheng. 2021. Improving large-scale language models and resources for Filipino. *arXiv preprint arXiv:2111.06053*.

Marie-Catherine De Marneffe, Christopher D Manning, Joakim Nivre, and Daniel Zeman. 2021. Universal dependencies. *Computational linguistics*, 47(2):255–308.

Wietse de Vries, Martijn Wieling, and Malvina Nissim. 2022. Make the best of cross-lingual transfer: Evidence from POS tagging with over 100 languages. In *Proceedings of the 60th Annual Meeting of the Association for Computational Linguistics (Volume 1: Long Papers)*, pages 7676–7685, Dublin, Ireland. Association for Computational Linguistics.

Matthew S Dryer and Martin Haspelmath. 2013. The world atlas of language structures online.

Juuso Eronen, Michal Ptaszynski, and Fumito Masui. 2023. Zero-shot cross-lingual transfer language selection using linguistic similarity. *Information Processing & Management*, 60(3):103250.

Harald Hammarström, Robert Forkel, and Martin Haspelmath. 2018. Glottolog 3.0. *Max Planck Institute for the Science of Human History*.

Ran Iwamoto, Hiroshi Kanayama, Alexandre Rademaker, and Takuya Ohko. 2021. A universal dependencies corpora maintenance methodology using downstream application. In *Proceedings of the Third Workshop on Computational Typology and Multilingual NLP*, pages 23–31.

Joo-Kyung Kim, Young-Bum Kim, Ruhi Sarikaya, and Eric Fosler-Lussier. 2017. Cross-lingual transfer learning for POS tagging without cross-lingual resources. In *Proceedings of the 2017 Conference on Empirical Methods in Natural Language Processing*, pages 2832–2838, Copenhagen, Denmark. Association for Computational Linguistics.

Bruce W Lee, Hyunsoo Cho, and Kang Min Yoo. 2023. Instruction tuning with human curriculum. *arXiv preprint arXiv:2310.09518*.

Paul Lewis. 2009. Ethnologue: Languages of the world.

Patrick Littell, David R Mortensen, Ke Lin, Katherine Kairis, Carlisle Turner, and Lori Levin. 2017. Uriel and lang2vec: Representing languages as typological, geographical, and phylogenetic vectors. In *Proceedings of the 15th Conference of the European Chapter of the Association for Computational Linguistics: Volume 2, Short Papers*, volume 2, pages 8–14.

LJ Miranda. 2023. Towards a Tagalog NLP pipeline.

Steven Moran and Daniel McCloy. 2019. Phoible 2.0. *Jena: Max Planck Institute for the Science of Human History*.

Fred Philippy, Siwen Guo, and Shohreh Haddadan. 2023. Identifying the correlation between language distance and cross-lingual transfer in a multilingual representation space. *arXiv preprint arXiv:2305.02151*.

Xipeng Qiu, Tianxiang Sun, Yige Xu, Yunfan Shao, Ning Dai, and Xuanjing Huang. 2020. Pre-trained models for natural language processing: A survey. *Science China Technological Sciences*, 63(10):1872–1897.

Edward P Stabler and Edward L Keenan. 2003. Structural similarity within and among languages. *Theoretical Computer Science*, 293(2):345–363.

A Appendix: Linguistic Distances from Filipino of the Top Performing Source Languages for XLM-R

Table 9: Linguistic distances from Filipino for the top 10 performing source languages, as determined by the XLM-R model's F1 score.

Lang	Fea	Gen	Geo	Inv	Pho	Synt
afr	0.63	1	0.54	0.49	0.59	0.75
heb	0.57	1	0.44	0.52	0.59	0.53
bul	0.55	1	0.47	0.55	0.36	0.60
vie	0.54	1	0.08	0.49	0.39	0.64
nor	0.80	1	0.49	0.66	0.59	0.68
urd	0.63	1	0.29	0.49	0.59	0.76
ces	0.62	1	0.50	0.47	0.59	0.72
pes	0.54	1	0.35	0.45	0.41	0.68
fao	0.80	1	0.52	0.66	0.59	0.68
eng	0.53	1	0.54	0.46	0.34	0.66

B Appendix: Linguistic Distances from Filipino of the Top Performing Source Languages for RoBERTa-Tagalog

Table 10: Linguistic distances from Filipino of the top 10 performing source languages, as determined by the RoBERTa-Tagalog model's F1 score.

Lang	Fea	Gen	Geo	Inv	Pho	Synt
eng	0.53	1	0.54	0.46	0.34	0.66
pcm	0.64	1	0.63	0.43	0.59	0.59
srp	0.78	1	0.48	0.66	0.86	0.65
glv	0.86	1	0.54	0.66	0.59	0.78
slv	0.58	1	0.51	0.47	0.59	0.63
spa	0.50	1	0.58	0.46	0.51	0.53
nld	0.63	1	0.52	0.53	0.59	0.71
hrv	0.65	1	0.50	0.46	0.59	0.89
pol	0.49	1	0.48	0.44	0.36	0.58
gle	0.53	1	0.56	0.45	0.59	0.54

C Appendix: Fertility Scores for UD Training Datasets

Table 11: Fertility scores for the training datasets of UD using XLM-R and RoBERTa-Tagalog as tokenizers (Part 1 of 2).

Language	XLM-R	RoBERTa-Tagalog
af	1.54	2.22
ar	1.13	2.58
be	2.16	6.17
bg	1.54	5.41
bxr	2.44	6.36
ca	1.38	1.93
cop	1.96	10.26
cs	1.72	3.33
cu	3.12	7.28
cy	1.56	2.38
da	1.47	2.34
de	1.56	2.68
el	1.65	9.24
en	1.32	1.63
es	1.34	1.94
et	1.82	2.83
eu	1.78	2.62
fa	1.36	6.60
fi	1.91	3.27
fo	1.58	2.25
fr	1.44	2.04
gd	1.67	2.26
gl	1.31	2.00
got	2.25	2.98
grc	3.27	10.36
gv	1.85	1.97
hbo	4.99	9.96
hi	1.30	8.49
hr	1.58	2.81
hsb	2.27	3.33
hu	1.75	3.41
hy	1.85	9.72
hyw	2.35	9.85
id	1.39	2.33
is	1.58	2.87
it	1.41	2.01

Table 12: Fertility scores for the training datasets of UD using XLM-R and RoBERTa-Tagalog as tokenizers (Part 2 of 2).

Language	XLM-R	RoBERTa-Tagalog
ja	1.20	1.49
kk	1.87	5.91
kmr	1.65	3.02
ko	2.12	8.11
koi	2.49	5.13
kpv	2.66	5.59
ky	1.83	7.12
la	1.61	2.22
lij	1.59	1.89
lt	1.82	3.32
lzh	1.96	3.06
mdf	2.35	5.13
mr	1.68	8.59
mt	2.29	2.77
myv	2.54	5.64
nl	1.48	2.23
no	1.48	2.36
olo	1.93	2.62
orv	2.44	5.77
pcm	1.22	1.41
pl	1.74	3.25
pt	1.38	2.08
qaf	1.93	2.30
qpm	2.03	2.68
qtd	1.40	2.45
ro	1.68	2.69
ru	1.63	5.68
sa	2.73	4.33
sk	1.75	2.84
sl	1.58	2.53
sme	2.55	3.25
sms	3.11	4.41
sr	1.60	2.73
sv	1.49	2.56
ta	2.10	20.86
te	1.94	13.50
tr	1.89	3.46
ug	2.19	9.77
uk	1.74	5.56
ur	1.32	6.28
vi	1.44	3.89
wo	1.81	2.05
zh	2.09	4.21

Author Index

Association for Computational Linguistics
209 N. Eighth Street
Stroudsburg, Pennsylvania 18360

ISBN 979-8-3313-0162-0

CURRAN ASSOCIATES INC.
proceedings.com